SPECTRUM

W9-CNJ-248

rade

6

ILLINOIS
Test Prep

Frank Schaffer Publications®

SPECTRUM

Frank Schaffer Publications®

Spectrum is an imprint of Frank Schaffer Publications.

Printed in the United States of America. All rights reserved. Except as permitted under the United States Copyright Act, no part of this publication may be reproduced or distributed in any form or by any means, or stored in a database or retrieval system, without prior written permission from the publisher, unless otherwise indicated. Frank Schaffer Publications is an imprint of School Specialty Publishing. Copyright © 2006 School Specialty Publishing.

Send all inquiries to:
Frank Schaffer Publications
8720 Orion Place
Columbus, Ohio 43240-2111

ISBN 0-7696-3486-9

3 4 5 6 7 8 9 10 MAZ 12 11 10 09 08 07

Table of Contents

Mathematics

What's Inside?

This workbook is designed to help you and your sixth grader understand what he or she will be expected to know on the Illinois sixth grade state tests. The state testing program measures student learning in different subject areas.

Practice Pages

The workbook is divided into a reading section and a mathematics section. Each section has practice activities that have questions similar to those that will appear on the state tests. Students should use a pencil to fill in the correct answers and to complete any writing on these activities.

Illinois Content Standards

Before each practice section is a list of the state standards covered by that section. The shaded *What it means* sections will help to explain any information in the standards that might be unfamiliar.

Mini-Tests and Final Tests

Practice activities are grouped by state standard. When each group is completed, the student can move on to a mini-test that covers the material presented on those practice activities. After an entire set of standards and accompanying activities are completed, the student should take the final tests, which incorporate materials from all the practice activities in that section.

Final Test Answer Sheet

The final tests have a separate answer sheet that mimics the style of the answer sheet the students will use on the state tests. The answer sheet appears at the end of each final test.

How Am I Doing?

The *How Am I Doing?* pages are designed to help students identify areas where they are proficient and areas where they still need more practice. Students can keep track of each of their mini-test scores on these pages.

Answer Key

Answers to all the practice activities, mini-tests, and final tests are listed by page number and appear at the end of the book.

Frequently Asked Questions

What kinds of information does my child have to know to pass the test?

The state of Illinois provides a list of the knowledge and skills that students are expected to master at each grade level. The practice activities in this workbook provide students with practice in each of these areas.

Are there special strategies or tips that will help my child do well?

The workbook provides sample questions that have content similar to that on the state tests. Test-taking tips are offered throughout the book.

How do I know what areas my child needs help in?

A special *How Am I Doing?* section will help you and your sixth grader evaluate progress. It will pinpoint areas where more work is needed as well as areas where your student excels.

Illinois Reading
Content Standards

The language arts section of the state test measures knowledge in reading.

Goal 1: Read with understanding and fluency.

Goal 2: Read and understand literature representative of various societies, eras, and ideas.

Illinois Reading
Table of Contents

© Frank Schaffer Publications

Reading Standards

Read with Understanding and Fluency

Goal 1: Read with understanding and fluency.

Learning Standard 1A—Students who meet the standard can apply word analysis and vocabulary skills to comprehend selections.

1. Identify and apply appropriate word analysis and vocabulary strategies (e.g., word patterns, structural analyses) to identify unfamiliar words. *(See page 8.)*
2. Use prefixes, suffixes, and root words to understand word meanings. *(See page 9.)*
3. Use synonyms and antonyms to express the implied meaning of a new word. *(See pages 10–11.)*

What it means:
- **Antonyms** are words with opposite meanings. For example, *sad* is an antonym for *happy*.
- **Synonyms** are words with similar meanings. For example, *cheerful* is a synonym for *happy*.

4. Determine the meaning of words in context using denotation and connotation strategies. *(See page 12.)*
5. Identify and interpret idioms, similes, analogies, and metaphors to express implied meanings of words. *(See pages 13–14.)*

What it means:
- **Similes**—using *like* or *as* to compare things that may seem unlike each other. Example: Her smile was as dazzling as the sun.
- **Metaphors**—comparing unlike things but without using *like* or *as*. Example: His body was a well-oiled machine.
- **Analogies**—making a comparison based on similarities between two things that are otherwise dissimilar.
- **Idioms**—using an expression that means something different from what it actually says.

6. Use etymologies to construct the meanings of new words. *(See page 15.)*
7. Apply appropriate word analysis, vocabulary, and contextual clues to determine the meaning of unfamiliar words across a range of subjects. *(See pages 16–17.)*
8. Recognize literary devices (e.g., figurative language, description, dialogue) in text. *(See page 18.)*

Learning Standard 1B *(See page 20.)*

Learning Standard 1C *(See page 48.)*

1A.1

Identifying Unknown Words

DIRECTIONS: Read each item. Choose the correct meaning for each underlined word.

1. The <u>passage</u> appeared in the magazine.
   - (A) exit
   - (B) crossing
   - (C) journey
   - (D) quotation

2. I <u>introduced</u> my dad to my teacher.
   - (F) proposed
   - (G) familiarized
   - (H) submitted
   - (J) suggested

3. The boat pulled up to the <u>landing</u>.
   - (A) touching down
   - (B) a dock
   - (C) the level part of a staircase
   - (D) taking off

4. The horses were <u>sheltered</u> in the barn.
   - (F) housed
   - (G) shielded
   - (H) concealed
   - (J) exposed

5. Karyn <u>registered</u> for the computer class.
   - (A) listed
   - (B) enlisted
   - (C) enrolled
   - (D) noticed

6. The poet led a <u>colorful</u> life.
   - (F) bright
   - (G) brilliant
   - (H) distinctive or unique
   - (J) multicolored

7. The deer was hidden in a <u>stand</u> of trees.
   - (A) a small retail business
   - (B) a raised platform
   - (C) holding a position
   - (D) a group of plants

8. Facts about antelopes were found in this <u>obscure</u> book.
   - (F) hide
   - (G) little-known
   - (H) baffling
   - (J) mysterious

9. The company <u>recalled</u> the cars because of safety concerns.
   - (A) repealed
   - (B) remembered
   - (C) reinstated
   - (D) summoned

STOP

© Frank Schaffer Publications

Name _____ Date _____

Word Meanings

DIRECTIONS: Choose a prefix from the Prefix Bank to add to a word from the Root Word Bank to form a word to fit the definition.

Prefix Bank	
pre-	de-
inter-	non-
re-	under-
dis-	over-
post-	in-

Root Word Bank	
-face	-protective
-arranged	-conformist
-value	-trust
-lock	-graduate
-considerate	-design

1. _____ means "set up beforehand."

2. _____ means "too protective."

3. _____ means "absence of trust."

4. _____ means "one who does not conform."

5. _____ means "to destroy the appearance of something."

6. _____ means "to treat as having little value."

7. _____ means "to lock together."

8. _____ means "continuing studies after graduating."

9. _____ means "careless of the rights or feelings of others."

10. _____ means "to change the design or appearance."

DIRECTIONS: Think of a new word for each of the prefixes below.

11. pre- _____

12. de- _____

13. inter- _____

14. non- _____

15. re- _____

16. under- _____

17. dis- _____

18. over- _____

19. post- _____

20. in- _____

STOP

© Frank Schaffer Publications

Reading

1A.3

Synonyms and Antonyms

DIRECTIONS: Read each item. Choose the answer that means the same or about the same as the underlined word.

 Clue   Look carefully at all the answer choices.

1. <u>tiresome</u> **job**
   - (A) hurried
   - (B) slow
   - (C) tedious
   - (D) dim

2. <u>arrogant</u> **man**
   - (F) heavy
   - (G) proud
   - (H) cunning
   - (J) humble

3. <u>surly</u> **individual**
   - (A) wild
   - (B) anxious
   - (C) gruff
   - (D) calm

4. <u>agile</u> **body**
   - (F) clumsy
   - (G) heavy
   - (H) nimble
   - (J) thin

5. <u>cheap</u> **gift**
   - (A) generous
   - (B) stingy
   - (C) expensive
   - (D) charitable

6. A <u>frank</u> answer is _____ .
   - (F) short
   - (G) honest
   - (H) long
   - (J) complicated

7. To be in the <u>midst</u> is to be in the _____ .
   - (A) center
   - (B) dark
   - (C) crowd
   - (D) outskirts

8. A person in <u>peril</u> is in _____ .
   - (F) clothing
   - (G) safety
   - (H) luck
   - (J) danger

9. To <u>thrive</u> is to _____ .
   - (A) withdraw
   - (B) wither
   - (C) prosper
   - (D) participate

10. An <u>ally</u> is a _____ .
   - (F) metal
   - (G) friend
   - (H) neighbor
   - (J) enemy

© Frank Schaffer Publications

DIRECTIONS: Read each item. Choose the word that means the opposite of the underlined word.

11. willing to leave

- (A) able
- (B) eager
- (C) reluctant
- (D) allowed

12. simple room

- (F) ornate
- (G) empty
- (H) full
- (J) unusual

13. dissimilar answers

- (A) identical
- (B) strange
- (C) unusual
- (D) unlike

14. The play commenced.

- (F) concluded
- (G) began
- (H) continued
- (J) failed

15. benign host

- (A) kind
- (B) spiteful
- (C) young
- (D) gracious

16. opened gingerly

- (F) carefully
- (G) carelessly
- (H) swiftly
- (J) gradually

17. absurd situation

- (A) ridiculous
- (B) horrible
- (C) funny
- (D) sensible

18. hoist the sails

- (F) lift
- (G) lower
- (H) display
- (J) mend

19. vacant room

- (A) clean
- (B) ancient
- (C) empty
- (D) inhabited

20. motivated worker

- (F) energized
- (G) uninspired
- (H) roused
- (J) new

STOP

Reading

1A.4

Denotative and
Connotative Meanings

DIRECTIONS: Choose the word with the more positive connotative meaning to complete each of the sentences below.

> **Example:**
>
> Mike *smirked* at me as he skated past.
>
> or
>
> Mike *grinned* at me as he skated past.
>
> *Smirked* has a more negative connotation than *grinned*, although the denotative meaning of each word is very similar.

Clue | The denotative meaning of a word is its actual meaning. The connotative meaning of a word is the positive or negative association that the word brings about.

1. The _____ (antique, old) dresser was battered in the move.

2. The weather in London was _____ (fine, wonderful) the whole time we were there.

3. Monica has some _____ (unique, strange) ideas about how to decorate for the party.

4. Jose's mother _____ (nagged, reminded) him about taking out the trash after dinner.

5. That's a(n) _____ (interesting, bizarre) choice of colors to put together.

6. Carly and Rich were _____ (arguing, discussing) the best way to spend the bonus check.

7. At just under five feet tall, Merrilee's grandmother is very _____ (short, petite).

8. Ted was _____ (furious, angry) when his package arrived dented and broken.

DIRECTIONS: Choose the word with the more negative connotative meaning to complete each of the sentences below.

9. The sandwiches were _____ (moist, soggy) after being in the cooler all day.

10. Jason's tuxedo was a(n) _____ (inexpensive, cheap) imitation of the designer original.

11. After two days without food, the castaways were _____ (starving, hungry).

12. The sinking of the luxury cruise ship was one of the worst _____ (disasters, accidents) in history.

STOP

© Frank Schaffer Publications

Name _____ Date _____

Interpreting Idioms

DIRECTIONS: An **idiom** is an expression that means something different from what it actually says. Each picture below illustrates an idiom in the story. Read the passage and then write what each idiom really means under the picture.

Last-Minute Stardom

It was time for the play to begin, but the lead actress had not arrived. When the door opened, everyone looked up expecting to see Beth.

"I hate to put a damper on things, but Beth has a fever and cannot possibly make it tonight," explained her mom.

"Well, I never put all my eggs in one basket," responded Ms. King. "Amanda has been our understudy for that part and knows it well. Amanda, put on Beth's costume."

Amanda was on cloud nine as she jumped off the stage after the performance and ran to where her family and friends were waiting at the back of the auditorium.

"You were terrific. You always were the apple of my eye," said Dad, as he gave Amanda a hug.

Amanda was speechless as everyone complimented her.

"What's the matter? Has the cat got your tongue?" asked her big brother.

"Speaking of cats," said Dad, "it's raining cats and dogs outside. Grandpa, you keep an eye on everyone while I run and get the car."

It seemed like an eternity before Dad returned. "Sorry it took so long. The traffic is slower than molasses in January. I avoided an accident in the parking lot only by the skin of my teeth."

"I get shotgun!" shouted Amanda's brother as they ran out to the car.

1. _____   2. _____   3. _____

4. **Choose another idiom from the story, and create a small picture to show what it actually says. Then write beside the picture what it really means.**

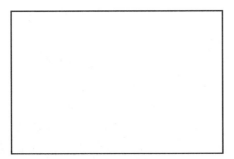

_____

_____

© Frank Schaffer Publications

Reading

1A.5

Using Analogies

DIRECTIONS: An **analogy** is a set of word pairs that have a particular kind of relationship. To solve the analogies below, determine how the first pair of words is related. Then choose a word from the Word Bank that correctly completes the analogy.

Word Bank

cloudless	red	permit	positive
melody	stop	untidy	foolish
light	land	come	lengthy
ordinary	lass	enjoy	century

1. *Quiet* is to *calm* as *silly* is to _____.

2. *Ten* is to *decade* as *hundred* is to _____.

3. *Foggy* is to *murky* as *clear* is to _____.

4. *Strange* is to *odd* as *usual* is to _____.

5. *Lavender* is to *purple* as *pink* is to _____.

6. *Liquid* is to *water* as *solid* is to _____.

7. *Cut* is to *sever* as *let* is to _____.

8. *Plain* is to *simple* as *song* is to _____.

9. *Out* is to *in* as *go* is to _____.

10. *Strong* is to *weak* as *heavy* is to _____.

11. *After* is to *before* as *go* is to _____.

12. *No* is to *yes* as *negative* is to _____.

13. *Boy* is to *girl* as *lad* is to _____.

14. *Smooth* is to *mussed* as *neat* is to _____.

15. *Grave* is to *flighty* as *short* is to _____.

16. *Enclosed* is to *open* as *dislike* is to _____.

STOP

© Frank Schaffer Publications

Name _____ Date _____

Using Etymologies

DIRECTIONS: Answer the following questions about foreign words used in English.

 Clue Many of the words we use in English are actually borrowed from other languages.

1. **Which of these words probably comes from a French word meaning *fair-haired*?**
   - (A) brunette
   - (B) blond
   - (C) petite
   - (D) critique

2. **Which of these words probably comes from a Spanish word meaning *the lizard*?**
   - (F) horse
   - (G) cat
   - (H) dog
   - (J) alligator

3. **Which of these is probably related to *skera*, an old Norse word meaning *to cut*?**
   - (A) shear
   - (B) scare
   - (C) share
   - (D) score

4. **Which of these words probably comes from a French word meaning *short*?**
   - (F) critique
   - (G) genre
   - (H) petite
   - (J) encore

5. **Which of these words probably comes from a German word meaning *preschool*?**
   - (A) encore
   - (B) patio
   - (C) kindergarten
   - (D) genre

6. **The French word *encore* means _____ .**
   - (F) again
   - (G) short
   - (H) type
   - (J) judgment

7. **Which of these words probably comes from the Middle English word *muflein* meaning *wrapped up*?**
   - (A) muffled
   - (B) mottled
   - (C) mounted
   - (D) molted

8. **Which of these words probably comes from the Middle English word *couchen* meaning *to lie down*?**
   - (F) cloud
   - (G) crowd
   - (H) catch
   - (J) crouch

STOP

© Frank Schaffer Publications

Name _____ Date _____

Using Context Clues to Determine Meaning

DIRECTIONS: Read the paragraph. Find the word that fits best in each numbered blank. Fill in the circle for the correct answer.

 Clue If you aren't sure which answer is correct, substitute each answer in the blank.

> People who travel or cross the Amazon and Orinoco rivers of South America are careful never to _____ **(1)** a foot or hand from the side of their boat. For just below the surface of these mighty waters _____ **(2)** a small fish feared throughout the _____ **(3)**. That fish is the flesh-eating piranha. It has a nasty _____ **(4)** and an even nastier _____ **(5)**. Although smaller fish make up most of its diet, the piranha will _____ **(6)** both humans and other animals.

1. Ⓐ lift
    Ⓑ dangle
    Ⓒ withdraw
    Ⓓ brush

2. Ⓕ lurks
    Ⓖ nests
    Ⓗ plays
    Ⓙ boasts

3. Ⓐ universe
    Ⓑ town
    Ⓒ continent
    Ⓓ village

4. Ⓕ habit
    Ⓖ friend
    Ⓗ flavor
    Ⓙ disposition

5. Ⓐ smile
    Ⓑ brother
    Ⓒ appetite
    Ⓓ memory

6. Ⓕ befriend
    Ⓖ bully
    Ⓗ attack
    Ⓙ analyze

STOP

© Frank Schaffer Publications

Name _____ Date _____

DIRECTIONS: Read the passage and answer the questions below.

Always running out of money? Have no idea where your money goes? Saving for a special trip, activity, or object? If you answered *yes* to any of these questions, it is time to plan a budget and stick to it.

Budgets have a bad rap as being too restrictive or too hard to follow. In reality, a budget can be very simple, and understanding how to use one can help you save for special things. There are three easy steps to follow.

The first step in building a livable budget is to record your spending habits. Look at your expenditures. Do you buy your lunch? Do you buy a soft drink or even water from a machine? You may discover you spend money foolishly. Buying a candy bar for $0.50 every day may seem insignificant, but by the end of the month, it adds up to $15.00. Instead, put a snack in your backpack.

The next step is determining your debits and credits. Look at what money comes in and what goes out. If you have determined your spending habits, you know what your debits are. Credits might be harder to determine if you do not have a job. Determine all the ways you get money. For example, count the dollars you earn or money given to you as presents. How much each week do you have available to spend? What are your sources of income?

If you do not have a regular source of income, you need to find ways to make money. Do you have an allowance? Can you negotiate with your parents to raise your allowance? Offer to do more chores or special jobs that will increase your income. Check out the neighborhood. Lawn work and baby-sitting are two jobs that you might like. Remember, your debits should not be more than your credits.

The last step is determining your cash flow and savings goals. How much money do you have available each week to spend? You might budget a small cash flow for yourself because you want to save for a new pair of skis, which means you might earn $10.00 a week, but only allow yourself to spend $3.00. Look at three important categories. How much money do you wish to save? How much money do you need for essentials? How much money do you want for frivolous activities? Determining the balance between savings goals and cash flow is an important decision for any budget.

7. **Define the following terms. Then, write the sentence or phrase that helped you determine its definition.**

expenditures

_____

_____

_____

debit

_____

_____

_____

credit

_____

_____

_____

cash flow

_____

_____

_____

STOP

© Frank Schaffer Publications

Reading

1A.8

Recognizing
Literary Devices

DIRECTIONS: This story is full of figurative language whose sounds make you think of what they mean, such as *zooming* and *fizzing*. Words like these are examples of **onomatopoeia**. Read the story and use the clues to write the correct word from the story on the line. Each word will be an example of onomatopoeia.

Summer Storm

Brian went zooming to the park on his bike. It started out as a perfect day, until Brian's mom made him drag his little brother Pete along.

"Wait for me, Brian," whined Pete as he tried to keep up.

Brian parked his bike and followed his nose to the concession stand. There were sizzling burgers on the grill, fresh-popped popcorn, and big barrels of fizzing root beer. He made his purchase and handed Pete his lunch. "Sit here and eat, and don't move until I come back to get you," Brian said.

As Pete began eating, he heard the pitter-patter of rain falling around him, but he stayed dry under the large tree. As the rain increased, the wind began to howl. With the leaves rustling above his head, it sounded as though it was raining harder. Then he heard the plink of the hail on the roof of the concession stand. When Pete saw lightning in the distance, he knew he should move from under the tree. Brian would just have to look for him.

When the storm got worse, Brian knew he had to find Pete. Brian thought he heard his name as he ran, but then wondered if it was the wind playing tricks on him. There it was again. "Brian!" That voice had never sounded so good.

1. moving rapidly

_____

_____

2. sharp metallic sound

_____

_____

3. soft crackling sound

_____

_____

DIRECTIONS: Answer the following questions.

4. What is the setting of this story?

_____

_____

5. Give two examples of dialogue from the story.

_____

_____

6. Give one example of a description from the story.

_____

_____

© Frank Schaffer Publications

Name _____ Date _____

Reading

1A

For pages 8–18

Read with
Understanding
and Fluency

Mini-Test 1

DIRECTIONS: Choose the best answer.

1. In which sentence does the word *grade* mean the same thing as in the sentence below?

   What grade did you get in math?

   A   This store offers only the top grade of fruits and vegetables.

   B   The best way to improve my grade is to study harder.

   C   The grade on this hill is so steep that trucks find it difficult.

   D   Mrs. Irwin will grade our papers today.

2. In which sentence does the word *point* mean the same thing as in the sentence below?

   Randi made her point by giving several examples.

   F   Grant broke the point on his pencil.

   G   The point of his argument is that the park is good for the town.

   H   The point of the compass changed as the boat made a turn.

   J   Can you point us in the right direction?

DIRECTIONS: Choose the answer that best defines the underlined part.

3. **pre**judge   **pre**school

   A   after

   B   less than

   C   more than

   D   before

4. cloudy   itchy

   F   much

   G   not

   H   about to become

   J   less

DIRECTIONS: Find the word that best completes each analogy.

5. Inhale is to exhale as tense is to _____ .

   A   breathe

   B   nervous

   C   gasp

   D   relaxed

6. Devastate is to destroy as renovate is to _____ .

   F   pulverize

   G   replant

   H   create

   J   remodel

7. Officer is to police force as soldier is to _____ .

   A   business

   B   uniform

   C   army

   D   commander

8. Eggs are to omelet as bread is to _____ .

   F   lunch

   G   sandwich

   H   cheese

   J   wheat

STOP

© Frank Schaffer Publications

Reading Standards

Read with Understanding and Fluency

Goal 1: Read with understanding and fluency.

Learning Standard 1A *(See page 7.)*

Learning Standard 1B—Students who meet the standard can apply reading strategies to improve understanding and fluency.

1. Use skimming to preview reading materials and scanning to detect major visual patterns and identify text structure before reading. *(See page 21.)*
2. Identify author's ideas and purposes. *(See pages 22–23.)*
3. Build and support plausible interpretations with evidence from the text through collaboration with others.
4. Make connections to real world situations or related topics before and during reading. *(See pages 24–25.)*
5. Identify main plot elements, conflicts, and themes in a variety of texts. *(See pages 26–27.)*
6. Distinguish between significant and minor details. *(See page 28.)*
7. Connect and clarify main ideas and concepts, and identify their relationship to other sources and topics. *(See pages 29–30.)*
8. Demonstrate an accurate understanding of important information in the text by focusing on the key ideas presented explicitly or implicitly. *(See page 31.)*
9. Demonstrate understanding of structure through the use of graphic organizers and outlining (e.g., mapping, time lines, Venn diagrams). *(See pages 32–33.)*
10. Apply survey strategies (e.g., use of bold print, organization of content, key words, graphics). *(See pages 34–35.)*
11. Summarize ideas from text to make and defend accurate inferences about character traits and motivations. *(See pages 36–37.)*
12. Interpret the meaning of figurative language in a variety of texts. *(See page 38.)*
13. Evaluate new information and hypotheses by comparing them to known information and ideas. *(See pages 39–40.)*
14. Apply self-monitoring and self-correcting strategies during reading to check and clarify for understanding. *(See pages 41–42.)*
15. Read aloud fluently (with expression, accuracy, and appropriate speed).
16. Develop creative interpretations of reading. *(See pages 43–44.)*
17. Select and read books for recreation. *(See page 45.)*

Learning Standard 1C *(See page 48.)*

© Frank Schaffer Publications

Name _____   Date _____

Reading

| 1B.1 |

Read with
Understanding
and Fluency

Skimming and Scanning a Passage

DIRECTIONS: Read the passage and answer the questions.

Clue

Skim the passage so you have an understanding of what it is about. Then skim the questions. Answer the easiest questions first, and then look back to the passage to find the answers.

The Special Gift

T.J. was poised to take a bite of his birthday cake when his mother said, "Not so fast, Mister. I think you have one more present coming."

"Really? What is it?" T.J. asked.

His father rose from his seat and walked around to T.J.'s chair. "Son, I have been waiting for this day to give you a very special gift. My father gave it to me when I was about your age, and it has been one of my most valued possessions. Now I want to give it to you." He then placed an old, dusty shoebox tied with string in front of T.J.

"This is my stamp collection, Son," his father began. "Your grandfather and I worked on it together. Now I want you to have it. I'll teach you about the different stamps and how to preserve them. We can go to the post office tomorrow after school, and you can pick out one of the new stamp sets to add to your collection."

T.J. tried to be excited about his gift, but he didn't understand what was so great about a box of old stamps. "Thanks, Dad," he said with a forced smile.

Then he noticed that Felicia had taken the box and was looking in each of the envelopes inside. "Look at this one!" she exclaimed. "It's from the year I was born. Hey, T.J., here's one from the year you were born, too!"

"That's right," said T.J.'s grandfather. "There are even stamps from my birthday!"

T.J. began to understand why the box was so important to his father and grandfather. He moved close to Felicia so that he could see the stamps better. Twenty minutes later, he didn't even notice that his ice cream was melted all over his cake.

1. **What is the main idea of this story?**
   - (A) Good manners are best.
   - (B) T.J. received a very special gift.
   - (C) Stamps are valuable.
   - (D) It's the thought that counts.

2. **When Felicia discovers the stamps from the years she and T.J. were born, what does T.J. begin to understand?**
   - (F) He and Felicia are about the same age.
   - (G) Some of the stamps are older than he is.
   - (H) The stamps are very meaningful.
   - (J) He was born after the collection was begun.

3. **Why didn't T.J. notice that his ice cream was melting?**
   - (A) He was no longer hungry.
   - (B) He was interested in the stamps.
   - (C) He did not like chocolate ice cream.
   - (D) He had already left the table.

4. **Who is the main character in this story?**
   - (F) Grandfather
   - (G) T.J.
   - (H) Father
   - (J) Felicia

STOP

Identifying the Author's Purpose

DIRECTIONS: Read the passage and then answer the questions on the next page.

Hi-Yo, Silver!

What did people do for entertainment before television? Today, the average child spends more time watching television than reading. Television is so much a part of daily life that many people cannot imagine what life was like before it.

Before television, there was radio. Radio was invented around 1916 from the telegraph. At first, it was used to get information quickly from one part of the country to another. By 1926, radios were common in homes. People listened to music, news, and shows in the same way we watch TV today.

Television was not invented until the 1940s, and it did not gain popularity in homes until 1955. Families gathered around their radios to listen to shows broadcast all over the world. One of the most popular radio shows was *The Lone Ranger.* This show was about a Texas Ranger and a faithful Native American, named Tonto, who tirelessly worked to stop evil.

The Lone Ranger rode a white horse named Silver and wore a black mask. The Lone Ranger hid his identity, because a gang that ambushed and killed five other Texas Rangers had left him for dead. He vowed to find these desperadoes. His white hat, white horse, black mask, and his famous call, "Hi-yo, Silver. Away!" became symbols of the American Wild West hero.

Other famous radio heroes were the Shadow and the Green Hornet. Eventually, radio shows became famous television shows as well. Comedians and vaudeville stars made the transition from the stage to radio to television. Comedians such as Jack Benny, Red Skelton, and George Burns had radio shows that became television favorites.

GO

© Frank Schaffer Publications

1. **What title best gives the main idea of this passage?**

   (A) *The Lone Ranger Rides Again*

   (B) *Before Television Came Radio*

   (C) *Radio Stars Hit It Big on TV*

   (D) *The History of Radio*

2. **What is not true of the passage?**

   (F) It gives a brief history of radio.

   (G) It tells about the transition from radio to television.

   (H) It focuses on *The Lone Ranger* show.

   (J) It shows how radio was far more popular than television.

3. **Which sentence below is an opinion?**

   (A) *The Lone Ranger* was the best radio show ever.

   (B) The Lone Ranger wore a white hat and black mask.

   (C) Tonto was the Lone Ranger's faithful companion.

   (D) *The Lone Ranger* took place in the American West.

4. **Which statement is true?**

   (F) Tonto rode a white horse named Silver.

   (G) Radio was invented in 1926.

   (H) Several radio shows later became popular TV shows.

   (J) Radio stars could not make it as television stars.

5. **Why do you suppose that *The Lone Ranger* was such a popular radio show?**

   (A) Families had nothing better to do with their free time.

   (B) It had the classic good guy against bad guys theme.

   (C) People liked the special effects.

   (D) People liked to watch the Lone Ranger and Tonto catch the bad guys.

6. **Why did the Lone Ranger wear a mask?**

   (F) He wanted to hide his true identity.

   (G) It was part of the Texas Ranger uniform.

   (H) To shield his eyes from the sun.

   (J) He wanted to be like his friend Tonto.

7. **What was the author's purpose for writing this passage?**

   (A) to entertain readers with stories about the Lone Ranger

   (B) to inform readers about the history of radio

   (C) to persuade readers to listen to the radio

   (D) to inform readers about famous radio heroes

STOP

Name _____   Date _____

Reading

1B.4

Making Connections
to Real-World Situations

**Read with
Understanding
and Fluency**

DIRECTIONS: Read the passage and then answer the questions on the next page that compare Antarctica and the Sahara.

Antarctica

Antarctica is the continent surrounding the South Pole. It contains 90 percent of the world's ice. Antarctica is the coldest and most desolate region on earth. It covers 5,400,000 square miles. Much of the land is buried under snow and ice one mile thick. The winter temperatures reach -100°F in the interior of the continent. On the coast, the temperatures fall below -40°F.

The interior of Antarctica is a frozen, lifeless region. The only animal life in Antarctica is found on the coastline or in the sea. Penguins, seals, whales, and other fish and birds live in or close to the coastal waters. These animals live on food from the sea.

The ancient Greeks called the North Pole the "Arctic." They believed that land at the South Pole must also exist. They called this supposed land "Antarctica," meaning the opposite of Arctic.

In 1928, Commander Richard E. Byrd of the U.S. Navy led a famous expedition to the South Pole. He and his men set up a base called Little America. Until his death in 1957, Byrd took five expeditions to Antarctica. He helped establish scientific research bases and led the largest Antarctic expedition in history with over 4,000 men and 13 ships.

The Sahara

Stretching almost 3,000 miles across North Africa, the Sahara Desert is an incredible natural wonder of sand, rock, and gravel. The Sahara covers over 3,500,000 square miles, which makes it by far the largest desert on earth. It extends west to east from the Atlantic Ocean to the Red Sea.

The name "Sahara" comes from an Arabic word, *Sahra*, which means *desert*. Because of the unusually low rainfall, the sun-scorched land and blistering winds make the Sahara the hottest region in the world during the summer. A sandy surface may reach a temperature of 170°F. The cloudless skies allow the daytime air temperature to reach 100°F. At night, the temperature often drops 40 to 50 degrees.

The Sahara's only vegetation is found near wells, springs, or streams. These fertile areas are called *oases*. Throughout the desert are many dry streambeds, called *wadis*. During a rare rain, they temporarily fill up with water. The Sahara supports some animal life, too––camels, lizards, and the addax, a desert antelope.

Some people of the Sahara live in tents, which allows them to move more easily in search of grassy areas. These people, called nomads, tend flocks of sheep, camels, or goats. Other people raise crops on land that has been irrigated.

GO

24

© Frank Schaffer Publications

1. **What challenges are presented by both regions because of their climate?**

_____

_____

_____

_____

_____

_____

_____

_____

_____

2. **How have humans and/or animals adapted to life in both regions?**

_____

_____

_____

_____

_____

_____

_____

_____

_____

_____

_____

_____

_____

3. **If you had to choose to go on an expedition to either Antarctica or the Sahara, which place would you choose? Why?**

_____

_____

_____

_____

_____

_____

_____

_____

_____

_____

_____

_____

_____

_____

_____

_____

_____

_____

_____

_____

_____

_____

_____

_____

_____

STOP

© Frank Schaffer Publications

Identifying Main Plot Elements

DIRECTIONS: Read the passage and then answer the questions on the next page.

By Saturday Noon

Saturday noon is one of those special times in our house. When I say special, I don't mean good special. By Saturday noon, my sisters and I need to have our bedrooms pristine.

When Dad inspects our rooms, he is like an army sergeant doing the white-glove test. If anything is out of place, if any clothes are left on the floor, and if your dresser isn't cleaned off and shiny, you don't get to go anywhere that day.

That isn't hard for Margaret. She's a neat freak. But Chelsea and I are normal, which is the problem—two normal sisters sharing a bedroom. On Monday, we start our separate piles: dirty clothes, wrinkled clothes, clothes we decided not to wear but forgot to hang up. By Wednesday, it's hard to find the floor. By Friday, the tops of the dressers are loaded. Plus, Mom won't let us throw everything down the laundry chute. "Sort it," she says.

Usually, we have enough time to get our clothes all folded and hung by noon, but last Saturday, Chelsea got sick. She spent the morning in the bathroom. I was left to clean the room alone. I had plans to shop with Jen.

At 10:00, Jen decided she wanted to leave early. I was desperate, so I shoved everything under Chelsea's bed, dusted the dressers, plumped the pillows, and called Dad for a room check.

Dad started his checklist. Everything was okay until Dad got to my closet. He turned and asked, "Where are all your clothes, Sara?"

"Dirty," I confessed.

Dad looked around until he spied the clothes under Chelsea's bed. "Dirty?" he asked.

I winced. "I must have missed those."

"Call Jen. You're not going shopping today," he said.

By Saturday noon, I was sick right alongside Chelsea. Mom said, "It's a good thing you didn't go shopping."

I figured it was just the opposite. If I had gone shopping, I would never have gotten sick.

GO

© Frank Schaffer Publications

1. **The words in the title "Saturday Noon" are used three times in the story. Why is that time important to Sara?**

   (A) Chelsea wanted to go shopping.

   (B) It was the deadline for having her room clean, which determined whether or not she could go out that day.

   (C) It was the time Sara had to have the laundry done.

   (D) It was when she got sick.

2. **How is Margaret different from Sara and Chelsea?**

   (F) She is older.

   (G) She is younger.

   (H) She is very neat.

   (J) She always goes out on Saturdays.

3. **What is the setting of this story?**

   (A) Sara's house

   (B) the mall

   (C) Chicago

   (D) Margaret's room

4. **Which of the following is not one of Sara's excuses for not getting her room clean?**

   (F) Sara's mom will not let her throw clothes down the laundry chute.

   (G) Chelsea got sick and couldn't help.

   (H) Jen wanted to leave early.

   (J) Her mom should clean her room.

5. **What is this story's plot?**

   (A) Sara can't wait to go shopping.

   (B) Sara knows she needs to have her room clean by Saturday noon, but blames everyone but herself for her room not being clean.

   (C) Sara allows her laundry to build up.

   (D) Sara's dad has unrealistic expectations for Sara.

6. **Which title below best fits this story?**

   (F) *The Blame Game*

   (G) *Cleaning Is Not Normal*

   (H) *Shopping with Jen*

   (J) *Laundry Woes*

STOP

Reading
1B.6

Distinguishing Between Significant and Minor Details

DIRECTIONS: Read the story and then look at the list of details from the story. Write an **S** on the line if the detail is significant to the meaning of the story; write an **M** if the detail is fairly minor to the meaning of the story.

Alex in Charge

Alex was thrilled. Mom and Dad were going to a movie, and she was allowed to babysit her sister Connie by herself. Connie was four. When their parents left, Alex and Connie sat down to watch a show on the family's brand-new TV. "We're watching my show because I'm in charge," said Alex. Connie burst into tears, stood right in front of the TV, and wouldn't move. "Fine. Then let's eat. But we're eating what I want because I am in charge."

Alex microwaved the leftover macaroni and cheese and gave some to Connie. Connie turned the bowl upside down all over her pink flowered dress. "You did that on purpose!" said Alex. "You are going to bed right now because I am in charge!" She carried a screaming Connie to the bedroom.

All of a sudden, Connie stopped crying. "What's that?" she said in a small, frightened voice. Alex listened and heard a strange noise. It sounded as if someone was climbing up the side of the house! Just then a huge, dark shadow fell across the room. Alex and Connie both screamed and held onto each other. They crept to the window in silence. They peered over the windowsill and saw a tree scratching against the pane. Sighing with relief, they both fell exhausted onto Connie's bed and went to sleep.

1. **Alex and Connie had leftover macaroni and cheese for dinner.** _____

2. **Alex had never babysat Connie before.** _____

3. **Mom and Dad were going to a movie.** _____

4. **Connie became frightened when she heard a strange noise.** _____

5. **Connie and Alex fell asleep together on Connie's bed.** _____

6. **Alex warmed up dinner in the microwave.** _____

7. **The family had a brand-new television set.** _____

8. **Connie was wearing a pink flowered dress.** _____

© Frank Schaffer Publications

Name _____ Date _____

Connecting Ideas

DIRECTIONS: Read the passage and then answer the questions on the next page.

Save the Elephants

Elephants are peaceful and magnificent animals. They live in social groups similar to families, with one female elephant, called a *matriarch*, leading the herd. As one of the largest land mammals in the world, African elephants have few predators. In fact, one of the greatest dangers to elephants in past years has not been from another animal but from humans. The value of the ivory tusks on the elephants was irresistible to greedy hunters.

African elephants that live on the grassy savanna have long, curved tusks. Some African elephants live in forest areas. They have shorter tusks, allowing them to move more freely through the crowded forest. Both male and female elephants have tusks, which they use as tools. Elephants tend to prefer either a right or left tusk, just as we favor our right or left hand. The tusk they use most often becomes shorter.

During the 1980s, the African elephant population was a casualty of human desires. The number of elephants declined from well over 1 million to about 600,000. It is estimated that more than 270 elephants were killed each day! Thousands of baby elephants, called *calves*, were left to take care of themselves. The African elephant was in a dangerous situation.

What was happening to the elephants? Poachers who wanted their ivory tusks were killing them. In many poor countries, poaching was one of the few ways to earn money. The ivory was valued around the world. It has been used for jewelry, statues, knife handles, billiard balls, piano keys, plus other products.

Organizations that protect animals and look out for their welfare were outraged. They devised a plan to alleviate the situation. They began a publicity campaign to spread awareness of the problem. Some large companies helped by refusing to buy ivory and asking their customers to do the same.

International laws were eventually passed to help make the killing of elephants less appealing. The sale of ivory was made illegal all around the world.

In recent days, "paintings" made by elephants have been used to raise money for elephant protection. Elephants use their trunks to hold the paintbrush. The paintings are then sold, with the money going toward conservation efforts.

© Frank Schaffer Publications

1. **What could you learn about elephants by looking at their tusks?**

_____

_____

_____

_____

2. **What do you think would have happened to the African elephant if no one had made any changes?**

_____

_____

_____

_____

_____

3. **What is a poacher?**

_____

_____

_____

_____

_____

4. **How do you think poachers were affected when ivory trade became illegal?**

_____

_____

_____

_____

_____

5. **What might happen to elephants if ivory trade were made legal again?**

_____

_____

_____

_____

_____

6. **What is the best way to continue to protect the elephants?**

_____

_____

_____

_____

_____

7. **Identify a real organization you know of that you believe would be likely to have prepared the story "Save the Elephants." Explain your selection.**

_____

_____

_____

_____

8. **Identify one other animal that needs to be "saved" in a way similar to the elephant. Briefly explain your answer.**

_____

_____

_____

_____

_____

© Frank Schaffer Publications

Understanding Implied Ideas

DIRECTIONS: Read the following letter and then answer the questions. You must read between the lines to get them all.

Write Me a Letter

Dear Mrs. Brewton,

Aloha from the big island! This state is so beautiful! We had the chance to drive fairly close to the volcano again this week, and then we went to a great luau. I'm learning a lot about the land, people, and wildlife here. I never thought I'd see some of the rocks and plants you talked about in class.

I've met a few more kids this past week. I've made a lot of friends since school ended last month in June. By the way, how are things in North Country? Any news from those friendly Americans to your south? The kids here think we only play hockey and race dogsleds. They were stunned to find out I love to kick the old ball around. I don't get to play fullback or goalie as much as I do back home, but it's still good practice for being on the team again next fall.

Say, before I forget, how is Fletch doing? Thanks for taking care of him while I'm gone. Let me know what you think of his coloring. It seems to me his green feathers are a bit less glossy than they should be. Although I miss him and he misses me (he does call me "Lady Love," you know), I know he's in good hands. Just don't teach him too many new words. His vocabulary is already greater than most of our class!

I'll see you next fall.
With great appreciation,
Chris

1. **Where is Chris living this summer?**

_____

_____

2. **How long has Chris been there?**

_____

_____

3. **Is Chris a boy or a girl?**

_____

_____

4. **What kind of pet does Chris own?**

_____

_____

5. **Where is Chris's home?**

_____

_____

6. **What sport does Chris play?**

_____

_____

STOP

Reading

Using Graphic Organizers

DIRECTIONS: Read the passage.

Decathlon

The decathlon is one of the most famous contests in sports. *Decathlon* is a Greek word that means "ten contests." The first decathlon was added to the Olympic Games in 1912. It was added in honor of athletes who competed in the original Olympic Games in Greece. Most of the games in the early Olympics were contests of running, jumping, and throwing. Today, these kinds of events are called track and field events.

A decathlon is a two-day contest that features ten separate events in track and field. The events for the first day are the 100-meter dash, long jump, shot put, high jump, and 400-meter run. The events for the second day are the 110-meter hurdles, discus throw, pole vault, javelin throw, and 1,500-meter run.

The 100-meter dash starts the decathlon. It takes just seconds for the athletes to run the 100-meter race, which is approximately the length of a football field.

An athlete has three chances for a high score in the long jump and high jump. The best score out of three attempts is used.

The shot put is an event that requires a tremendous amount of power to throw a 16-pound metal ball, called a *shot*, as far as possible.

The final event of the first day is the 400-meter run. This race is almost a quarter of a mile in length. It is a hard race to run because it is too long to run in one burst of energy. But it is too short to run at a slower pace. Some people have called this the "murderous race."

The second day begins with the 110-meter hurdles. The runners must not only run fast, but also jump over ten hurdles, which are three-and-a-half feet tall.

The discus throw is an event in which an athlete throws a four-pound metal plate, called a *discus*, as far as possible.

The pole vault is one of the hardest events of the decathlon. An athlete runs and lifts himself or herself high into the air on a pole. The aim is to jump over a high bar without knocking it down.

The javelin throw event requires an athlete to throw a javelin, a kind of spear, as far as possible.

The final event is the 1,500-meter run. It is a little less than a mile long. The goal of every decathlon athlete is to win the gold medal in the Olympic Games. The winner is often called "the world's greatest athlete."

GO

© Frank Schaffer Publications

Name _____ Date _____

DIRECTIONS: Complete the charts below to summarize the events of the decathlon.

Decathlon Events by Day

First Day	Second Day
1.	6.
2.	7.
3.	8.
4.	9.
5.	10.

Name of Events	Description
11.	An athlete throws a four-pound metal plate as far as possible.
12.	This race is approximately the length of a football field. It takes just seconds to run.
13.	An athlete jumps over a high bar by using a pole to lift himself or herself into the air.
14.	An athlete has three chances to make his or her highest jump.
15.	This is the final event of the second day. The race is a little less than a mile.
16.	An athlete throws a 16-pound metal ball as far as possible.
17.	While running, an athlete jumps over ten hurdles that are three-and-a-half feet tall.
18.	An athlete throws a special spear as far as possible.
19.	The longest jump out of three attempts is used.
20.	This race is the final event of the first day.

STOP

Reading

1B.10

Applying Survey Strategies

DIRECTIONS: Read the passage and then answer the questions on the next page.

Get a Horse!

Before automobiles were common, American roads looked very different than they do today. Most roads were filled with horses pulling carts or carriages.

Gasoline-powered automobiles were available only to a few wealthy individuals before the early 1900s. The sight of early motor cars was exciting to the American public. People ran out into the streets to see the "horseless carriage."

Not everyone welcomed the first automobiles. They were hard to start and difficult to drive. Cars were very noisy. They frightened horses and spewed dust clouds into the air. Some people would shout, "Get a horse!" at automobile drivers. Indeed, at the time, it did seem that owning a predictable, friendly horse and a comfortable carriage was better than the unpredictable mechanical car.

Taking a car trip—whether it was down the road or across the state—was quite a challenge in those early days. Hours of preparation were needed. Every part of the car had to be checked and cleaned. Drivers had to bring their own gas, oil, and tools because there were no gas stations along the way if they broke down. Travelers also had to pack their own food. There were no signs, traffic lights, or speed limits, so drivers had to be very careful and know their way.

Early automobiles were not enclosed; they had open tops. Motorists wore coats, goggles, and hats, but often these were not enough to protect them from the elements. If the weather was rainy or particularly cold, a car ride could be unpleasant or even impossible. Motorists often came home very dirty.

As time went on, cars became more and more popular. Driving became cheaper, safer, and easier. And the enclosed tops made it possible to drive in comfort in all kinds of weather.

Today's cars are more varied, comfortable, and fun to drive. Modern cars come in different colors, shapes, and sizes. People can choose a car that fits their individual tastes and preferences. Some drivers use computers, CD players, and telephones in their cars. Some cars run on electricity or solar power. Things certainly have changed since the early days of the automobile. Now, instead of horses, the streets are filled with cars.

GO

© Frank Schaffer Publications

1. To what does <u>horseless carriage</u> refer in the passage?

   Ⓐ   the American public

   Ⓑ   people

   Ⓒ   streets

   Ⓓ   early motor cars

2. What <u>spewed dust clouds into the air</u>?

   Ⓕ   cars

   Ⓖ   horses

   Ⓗ   people

   Ⓙ   streets

3. To what does <u>quite a challenge</u> refer?

   Ⓐ   hours of preparation

   Ⓑ   dusty streets

   Ⓒ   taking a car trip

   Ⓓ   crossing the state

4. To what does <u>unpleasant</u> refer?

   Ⓕ   weather

   Ⓖ   rain

   Ⓗ   car ride

   Ⓙ   cold

5. To what does <u>fun</u> refer?

   Ⓐ   today's cars

   Ⓑ   varied

   Ⓒ   comfort

   Ⓓ   driving

6. Which of the following would make a good heading before the fourth paragraph?

   Ⓕ   The Invention of the Automobile

   Ⓖ   Early Automobile Travel

   Ⓗ   Automobile Production

   Ⓙ   Early Public Reaction to the Automobile

7. Which of the following would make a good heading before the very last paragraph?

   Ⓐ   The Modern Automobile

   Ⓑ   Buying Your First Car

   Ⓒ   Cars and Traffic

   Ⓓ   The Rise of Imported Autos

8. How does the art accompanying the article give you a clue about the information the article will contain?

   _____

   _____

   _____

   _____

   _____

   _____

   _____

   _____

   _____

   _____

STOP

Analyzing Characters

DIRECTIONS: Read the story.

Slumber Party

It was the night Annabel had looked forward to for weeks. Four girls were arriving for a sleepover party! She had asked her parents many times, and finally they said *yes*. Annabel nervously wandered around the house, waiting for her guests to arrive. Finally, four cars pulled up and the doorbell rang.

Annabel threw open the door and welcomed her guests. The girls piled into Annabel's house in a jumble of sleeping bags and overnight cases.

"Thank you for inviting me," Robin said. "I brought you a thank-you gift." She held a small box out to her hostess.

"Yum! Chocolates!" Sheila shouted. She grabbed the box and shoved a candy into her mouth. She dropped the empty wrapper on the floor. "Got any milk?" she said, with her mouth full.

"There's milk in the kitchen," Annabel said as she pointed the way. Then, she noticed that another one of her guests did not look happy. "Tamiko, what's wrong?"

"I've never slept away from home," Tamiko admitted. "I'm a little nervous. My mother said I could call home if I needed to."

"You'll be all right," Annabel reassured her. "But you can use the phone anytime. It's right over there . . . hey? Where's the phone?" She looked at the empty table. Her eyes followed the telephone cord to a corner of the room. A girl was talking animatedly into the phone. It was the last guest, Paula.

"Is it okay if my friend Dan comes over?" Paula called over to Annabel. "He says he's bored."

"No!" Annabel responded, a little shocked. "There are no boys at this slumber party. Well, except for my kid brother, Ted."

"Oh." Paula rolled her eyes and went back to chatting on the phone.

"I brought a flashlight and a teddy bear," Tamiko showed the girls. "They'll help me feel better in the middle of the night."

"I'll put my sleeping bag next to yours," Robin told her. "I hope that makes you feel safer."

"Don't worry," Annabel smiled. "There's nothing to be afraid of!"

"Oh, yeah?" Ted chuckled to himself from his hiding place at the top of the staircase. Annabel's brother was wearing a horrible monster mask, and he carried a plastic ax. "Just wait until I jump into their room at midnight!"

GO

© Frank Schaffer Publications

DIRECTIONS: Pick a word from the Word Bank to describe each of the characters. Write two examples from the story that prove why your description fits each person.

Word Bank

fearful	greedy	polite
gracious	mischievous	rude

Example:

Annabel is <u>gracious</u>.

    A.   She says "Welcome!" to her guests.

    B.   She shows her friends where the milk and the phone are when she's asked.

1. Robin is _____ .

    A. _____

        _____

    B. _____

        _____

2. Sheila is _____ .

    A. _____

        _____

    B. _____

        _____

3. Tamiko is _____ .

    A. _____

        _____

    B. _____

        _____

4. Paula is _____ .

    A. _____

        _____

    B. _____

        _____

5. Ted is _____ .

    A. _____

        _____

    B. _____

        _____

STOP

Reading

1B.12

Interpreting the Meaning of Figurative Language

DIRECTIONS: Read the passages and answer the questions.

from *Annabel Lee*
And neither the angels in Heaven above
   Nor the demons down under the sea,
Can ever dissever my soul from the soul
   Of the beautiful Annabel Lee

1. **In the poem, Annabel Lee is a maiden who lived in a kingdom by the sea. Tell how the third line of the passage might make you think of the sea.**

   _____

   _____

   _____

2. **Which of the following types of figurative language is present in the third line of the passage?**

   (A) personification

   (B) alliteration

   (C) idiom

   (D) simile

from *My Love Is Like a Cherry*
My love is like a cherry that has no stone;
My love is like a chicken that has no bone;
My love is like a story that has no end;
My love is like a baby with no cryin'.

3. **How does the figurative language in this passage make you think of love? Describe how the images make you feel.**

   _____

   _____

   _____

   _____

4. **Which of the following types of figurative language is present in the third line of the passage?**

   (F) simile

   (G) onomatopoeia

   (H) analogy

   (J) alliteration

Source: "Annabel Lee," by Edgar Allan Poe, from *Anthology of American Literature, Volume 1: Colonial Through Romantic,* New York: Macmillan, 1980, pp. 931–932.

© Frank Schaffer Publications

Name _____ Date _____

Comparing New Information with Personal Knowledge

DIRECTIONS: Read the passage and then answer the questions on the next page.

An Inferencing Incident

"Quiet down, students, and please go to your desks," Mr. Chan said to the class. He waited for everyone to get settled. "Now, please take out your writing journals. Today, we will be learning about inferencing."

"Is that like conferencing?" Daphne asked eagerly. The students often held conferences to discuss their stories, and Daphne had just finished a good one.

"No," replied Mr. Chan. "But that's a good guess. In fact, that's what inferencing is—it is making an educated guess based on what you already know. Then, you add to it any new information you receive. Daphne saw that we were using our journals and inferred that we would be doing something that involved writing. Good inferencing, Daphne!"

Just then, a loud clanging noise rang through the room. The students put down their materials and lined up at the door. They walked single file out to the playground. All the other students soon joined them. This had happened many times before, so the students knew what to do.

After waiting a long time on the playground, the restless students began to wonder. They usually did not have to wait this long before returning to their classrooms. All at once, a red truck with a ladder on top drove up to the school.

The students began talking anxiously. Some men and women raced around to the side of the building carrying a water hose. The students became nervous as they saw the men and women direct the hose to where a small puff of smoke was coming out of a window near the school's cafeteria. Mr. Chan went to talk with the principal as the students watched in concern.

"Don't worry," Mr. Chan reassured them a moment later. "Everyone is safe. The situation will be taken care of shortly. But I'm going to make an inference. I infer that we may be eating lunch in our classroom today instead of in the cafeteria!"

GO

© Frank Schaffer Publications   **39**

Name _____ Date _____

DIRECTIONS: Choose each correct choice, and then answer the questions. Use your own knowledge and experiences to help you answer.

1. **At the beginning of the article, the students are _____ .**

   Ⓐ quietly working on an assignment

   Ⓑ out of their desks and making noise

   Ⓒ working on a science experiment

   How do you know?

   _____

   _____

   _____

2. **Daphne feels _____ her finished story.**

   Ⓕ proud and excited to share

   Ⓖ dissatisfied with

   Ⓗ ashamed of

   How do you know?

   _____

   _____

   _____

3. **The loud noise is _____ .**

   Ⓐ the children misbehaving

   Ⓑ a fire alarm

   Ⓒ a thunderstorm

   What are the clues?

   _____

   _____

   _____

4. **The people who arrive at the school are _____ .**

   Ⓕ police officers

   Ⓖ firefighters

   Ⓗ a TV crew

   What are the clues?

   _____

   _____

   _____

5. **The smoke is most likely caused by _____ .**

   Ⓐ burnt pizza

   Ⓑ a science experiment

   Ⓒ library books burning

   How do you know?

   _____

   _____

   _____

6. **Explain why Mr. Chan says the students would be eating their lunch in the classroom.**

   _____

   _____

   _____

   _____

   _____

   _____

STOP

© Frank Schaffer Publications

Applying
Self-Monitoring Strategies

DIRECTIONS: Read the passage and then answer the questions on the next page.

Read the questions first. Think about them as you read the passage.

From Dreams to Reality

People have probably always dreamed of flight. As they watched birds fly, they wished that they could soar into the blue sky. As they watched the night sky, they wished they could explore the distant bright specks called *stars*. These dreams led inventors and scientists to risk their lives to achieve flight.

Orville and Wilbur Wright's first flight at Kitty Hawk in 1903 was only the beginning. Flight continued to improve and dreams soared further into space. The first manned space flight occurred in 1961 when Russian cosmonaut Yuri A. Gagarin orbited the earth a single time. In 1963, the first woman cosmonaut, Valentina Tereshkova, orbited the earth 48 times.

The Russians led the race for many years. In 1965, another cosmonaut, Alesksei A. Leonov, took the first space walk. In 1968, the Russians launched an unmanned spacecraft that orbited the moon. The pictures that returned to earth encouraged man to take the next step to land on the moon.

The United States became the leader in the space race when *Apollo 11* landed on the moon in 1969. Neil Armstrong was the first man to step on the lunar surface. As he did so, he said these famous words, "That's one small step for a man, one giant leap for mankind." Later in 1969, Charles Conrad, Jr., and Alan L. Bean returned to the moon. In 1972, the United States completed its last mission to the moon, *Apollo 17*.

Today people continue their quest for space, gathering data from the Mir Space Station, which was launched in 1986. In addition, unmanned probes have flown deep into space toward the planets, sending back pictures and scientific readings.

GO

© Frank Schaffer Publications

1. **What is this passage mainly about?**

   (A) famous cosmonauts

   (B) a brief history of human flight

   (C) the first flight

   (D) the space race

2. **What happened first?**

   (F) The Mir Space Station was launched.

   (G) Yuri Gagarin orbited the earth a single time.

   (H) Neil Armstrong walked on the moon.

   (J) The first woman orbited the earth.

3. **Why do you suppose the race to achieve firsts in space travel was so important?**

   (A) It prompted the United States to excel.

   (B) It encouraged cooperation between the two countries.

   (C) It discouraged people from being interested in space travel.

   (D) It developed fierce rivalry that led to many mistakes.

4. **Which of these is an opinion?**

   (F) The United States became the leader in the space race with the first landing on the moon.

   (G) All people have dreamed about being able to fly.

   (H) Today unmanned space probes explore space.

   (J) The Russians led the space race for several years.

5. **What is the purpose of this passage?**

   (A) to inform

   (B) to advertise

   (C) to entertain

   (D) to promote an idea

6. **Which statement is false?**

   (F) The first woman in space was Valentina Tereshkova.

   (G) The first landing on the moon was in 1969.

   (H) Russia achieved the first manned space flight.

   (J) The last landing on the moon in 1972 ended the space race.

7. **Who was the first man to step on the moon?**

   (A) Yuri Gagarin

   (B) Orville Wright

   (C) Neil Armstrong

   (D) Alan Bean

STOP

© Frank Schaffer Publications

Name _____   Date _____

Reading

1B.16

Read with
Understanding
and Fluency

Developing
Creative Interpretations

DIRECTIONS: Read the poem and then answer the questions on the next page.

A Doomed Romance

You are my love, my love you are.
I worship you from afar;
I through the branches spy you.

You, Sir, are a climbing thug.
I do not like your fuzzy mug.
Away from me, please take you!

Oh, grant me peace, my love, my dove.
Climb to my home so far above
This place you call your warren.

I like my home in sheltered hollow
Where fox and weasel may not follow.
Please go away, tree rodent!

I love your ears, so soft and tall.
I love your nose, so pink and small.
I must make you my own bride!

I will not climb, I cannot eat
The acorns that you call a treat.
Now shimmy up that oak; hide!

Now I hide up in my bower.
Lonesome still, I shake and cower.
Sadness overtakes me.

I must stay on the lovely ground
With carrots crisp and cabbage round.
I long for gardens, not trees.

© Frank Schaffer Publications

1. **Who are the two speakers in this ballad? Identify them and write one adjective to describe the tone of each voice.**

   A. _____

   _____

   B. _____

   _____

2. **Briefly, what story does the poem tell? Explain in one complete sentence.**

   _____

   _____

   _____

   _____

   _____

   _____

3. **What do you think the theme of this poem is? Write it in one phrase or sentence.**

   _____

   _____

   _____

   _____

   _____

   _____

   _____

4. **Circle two adjectives to describe the first speaker in the poem.**

angry	lovesick
happy	hopeful	silly

5. **Circle two adjectives to describe the second speaker in the poem.**

joyful	relaxed
annoyed	realistic	happy

6. **Explain how the first speaker tries to make his home appealing to his love. Write in complete sentences.**

   _____

   _____

   _____

   _____

7. **Where does the second speaker live? How does it differ from where the first speaker lives? Write in complete sentences.**

   _____

   _____

   _____

   _____

STOP

© Frank Schaffer Publications

Finding a Favorite

DIRECTIONS: What do you like to read? From the library, borrow a fiction, nonfiction, biography, and poetry book. Read them and write a brief summary of each.

1. **Title of fiction book** _____ .

   Summary: _____

   _____

   _____

   _____

   _____

2. **Title of nonfiction book** _____ .

   Summary: _____

   _____

   _____

   _____

   _____

3. **Title of biography** _____ .

   Summary: _____

   _____

   _____

   _____

   _____

4. **Title of poetry book** _____ .

   Summary: _____

   _____

   _____

   _____

   _____

5. **What are the main differences in the books you chose?**

   _____

   _____

   _____

   _____

   _____

6. **In what ways are the books you chose the same?**

   _____

   _____

   _____

   _____

   _____

7. **Which type of book did you like the most? Why?**

   _____

   _____

   _____

   _____

   _____

   _____

   _____

STOP

© Frank Schaffer Publications

Mini-Test 2

DIRECTIONS: Read the story and then answer the questions on the next page.

Bonkers for Baseball

I remember a special Mother's Day back in 1939. My mom was a big baseball fan so my father treated us to tickets for the Brainford Bisons game. We sat in box seats owned by my father's company. It was an exciting day.

Before the game began, we started talking to a woman sitting in a nearby box seat. We learned that she was the mother of the Beulah Blaze's pitcher. Her son, Brian Falls, had been pitching in the minor leagues for three years. This was the first time she had ever seen him pitch in a professional game.

For the special event, Brian Falls had treated his mother to a box seat. He had the box decorated in flowers. Mrs. Falls was so excited. She told us that she had always encouraged Brian to become a baseball player. Her dream for her son had come true.

My team wasn't doing very well in the early innings. With Brian Falls pitching, the Brainford Bisons' batters kept striking out. Then, Falls threw a fastball to the plate. The batter swung at it. He caught a piece of it and fouled it off. The foul ball flew into the crowd. It came straight toward us! My dad and I reached into the air to catch it, but the ball veered left and hit Mrs. Falls in the head. She was knocked unconscious. We couldn't believe it—out of all the people in the stands, the ball hit the pitcher's mother! Mrs. Falls was rushed to the hospital. For the rest of the game we wondered what had happened to her. Later we learned the rest of the story.

Brian Falls left the game to accompany his mom to the hospital. He was so upset that he told her he would quit the game. His mother, who was recovering nicely, convinced him to stay in baseball. It's a good thing, because 3 years later he joined the major leagues.

© Frank Schaffer Publications

1. **What would be another good title for this story?**

   (A) *Mother's Day at the Ballpark*

   (B) *Making It in the Majors*

   (C) *Brian Falls: His Career in Baseball*

   (D) *The Brainsford Bisons Steal Home*

Here is a time line of what happens in the story.

The family goes to the baseball game for Mother's Day.

A foul ball is hit into the stands.

Brian Falls joins the major leagues.

2. **Which of these events should go in the empty box?**

   (F) Mrs. Falls convinces Brian not to quit baseball.

   (G) Mrs. Falls is taken to the hospital.

   (H) The family discovers that the woman they've been talking with is the mother of the Beulah Blaze's pitcher.

   (J) The ball is almost caught by the narrator.

3. **Why do you suppose Brian Falls had his mother's box seat decorated with flowers?**

   (A) because he wanted to impress his friends

   (B) because it was the first time she had seen him pitch professionally

   (C) because he was in the major leagues

   (D) because she told him not to quit

4. **Why was Mrs. Falls taken to the hospital?**

   (F) because she needed to tell Brian to stay in the game

   (G) because she was a nurse

   (H) because she was sick

   (J) because she was hit by a foul ball

5. **Mrs. Falls probably taught Brian to _____ .**

   (A) follow his dreams

   (B) give up when things got too hard

   (C) play baseball

   (D) fight against his opponents

6. **From reading the passage, how do you suppose the narrator feels about baseball?**

   (F) He thinks it's a silly game.

   (G) He despises it.

   (H) He is bored with it.

   (J) He enjoys it.

STOP

© Frank Schaffer Publications

Reading Standards

Read with Understanding and Fluency

Goal 1: Read with understanding and fluency.

Learning Standard 1A *(See page 7.)*

Learning Standard 1B *(See page 20.)*

Learning Standard 1C—Students who meet the standard can comprehend a broad range of reading materials.

1. Confirm, reject, and modify questions, predictions, and hypotheses based on evidence in text. *(See pages 49–50.)*
2. Use relevant and accurate references, most of which are specific and fully supported to make generalizations from content. *(See page 51.)*
3. Ask and respond to open-ended questions. *(See pages 52–53.)*
4. Compare the theme, topic, text structure, and story elements of various selections within a content area. *(See page 54.)*
5. Interpret concepts or make connections through analysis, evaluation, inference, and/or comparison. *(See pages 55–56.)*
6. Select reading strategies for text appropriate to the reader's purpose. *(See page 57.)*
7. Recognize how reader response is related to text interpretation. *(See pages 58–59.)*
8. Identify the author's controlling idea/thesis. *(See pages 60–61.)*
9. Interpret imagery and figurative language (e.g., alliteration, metaphor, simile, personification). *(See page 62.)*

What it means:
- **Figurative language** is language used for descriptive effect. It describes or implies meaning, rather than directly stating it.

10. Explain how illustrators use art to express their ideas. *(See page 63.)*
11. Recognize how illustrations from various cultures reflect, interpret, and enhance the text.
12. Recognize the influence media (e.g., television, film) can have on the reader's point of view concerning fiction materials. *(See page 64.)*
13. Apply appropriate reading strategies to fiction and nonfiction texts within and across content areas. *(See page 65.)*

© Frank Schaffer Publications

Reading

1C.1

Making and
Refining Predictions

DIRECTIONS: Before reading the story, look at the sentences on the next page and write **F** beside those you think are facts. Write **O** if you think the statements are opinions. Then read the story and answer the statements again. Has the story changed your thinking about wolves?

Wolf Ways

Wolves are often pictured in fairy tales as ferocious animals, always ready to attack and kill anything they can catch. The Three Little Pigs flee from the "big, bad wolf." Little Red Riding Hood must beware of the wolf that dresses up like Grandma and wants to eat her. But are wolves really that vicious?

Wolves are social animals and live together in packs of anywhere from two or three to twenty wolves. Each pack has a male and a female leader called the *alpha wolves*. The leaders are usually the strongest and healthiest animals. Usually, only the alpha female has cubs. The members of a pack generally cooperate and get along with one another.

Wolves are often pictured howling at the moon. Scientists have discovered that the howl is actually a way of locating other wolves, assembling the pack, sounding an alarm, or announcing a kill. Besides their howl, wolves use body language to communicate. The position of their back, neck, ears, and tail send distinct messages that other wolves understand. A wolf with its ears and tail up is high-ranking. A wolf with its tail down is showing submission.

Because they are hunters, wolves have a strong sense of smell, much greater than a human's sense of smell. That means they can smell their prey while it's still far away, and they also know where their enemies are. Wolves use smell to mark the edges of their territory. This tells other wolves to stay away.

Wolves usually feed on large animals such as deer and elk, with the pack working together to bring down their prey. They kill only when they are hungry and need to eat.

Who are the worst enemies of wolves? Humans! Wolves are more likely to run from a person than to attack, but because of their ferocious reputation, they have been hunted and killed for years. Wolves were once common across much of North America, but they are now rare and can be found only in remote wooded regions.

GO

© Frank Schaffer Publications

Name _____ Date _____

1. _____   Wolves are big, bad, and ferocious.   _____

2. _____   Wolves live in packs.   _____

3. _____   I'd like to find a wolf in my yard.   _____

4. _____   A wolf pack is very large.   _____

5. _____   Members of wolf packs usually cooperate with one another.   _____

6. _____   Wolves like to howl at the moon.   _____

7. _____   A wolf's howl communicates a message to other wolves.   _____

8. _____   Wolves have a strong sense of smell.   _____

9. _____   Wolves hunt large animals.   _____

10. _____ Elk tastes better to a wolf than other animals.   _____

11. _____ When a wolf has its tail down, it is communicating a message   _____
                  to other wolves.

12. _____ Wolves are scary animals.   _____

DIRECTIONS: Predict what will happen to wolves in the United States. Support your prediction with facts from the article.

13. _____

    _____

    _____

    _____

    _____

STOP

                                        © Frank Schaffer Publications

Name _____ Date _____

Reading

1C.2

Read with
Understanding
and Fluency

Citing Evidence
for Support

DIRECTIONS: Read the passage and then answer the questions.

The Flying Congressman

The first major battle of the Civil War was fought near the small town of Manassas Junction, Virginia. The Union army called the battle Bull Run, after the creek by that name. Inasmuch as this quaint little town lay just 30 miles southwest of Washington, D.C., a number of citizens from the nation's capital thought it might be fun to pack a picnic lunch, load up the family, and take a buggy ride out to watch the Confederates "get what was coming to them." They viewed the upcoming battle as nothing more than a sporting event. Even members of Congress were in attendance. No fewer than six senators and an undetermined number of congressmen showed up, as did pretty ladies in fancy gowns, all traveling in style in expensive buggies and carriages.

One particular congressman provided what turned out to be the only entertainment of the day for the spectators from the big city. What was predicted to be an easy victory for the Union forces turned into a rout. Federal troops retreated to the capital at a record pace, followed by carriages of Washington's elite—minus their picnic baskets. These were discarded when the rout began, and the Confederate soldiers had a feast when the battle was over.

Although those in flight were preoccupied with their safety, they could not help noticing a tall, long-legged congressman who, on foot, was leading the pack in its frantic race back to the capital. He was seen jumping ditches and gullies, and was said to have cleared a six-foot fence with a foot to spare. Many of the terror-stricken refugees howled with laughter, despite their fear.

History does not relate the name of the fleet and agile congressman. But there is a chance he might be the same legislator who, after reaching the safety of the capital, was confronted by President Lincoln. The President glared at the panting legislator and is supposed to have said dryly, "I congratulate you on winning the race!"

---

1. **This story mostly shows that _____ .**

   (A) many people died at the Battle of Bull Run

   (B) congressmen during the Civil War were quite athletic

   (C) some people in Washington, D.C., did not take the beginning of the Civil War seriously

   (D) the Confederates would win the war

2. **Cite specific evidence from the text to support your answer to question 1.**

   _____

   _____

   _____

3. **Why did the spectators run away from the battle?**

   (F) because the Union soldiers were winning the battle

   (G) because they had lost their picnic baskets

   (H) because they were in buggies

   (J) because the Union soldiers were losing the battle

4. **Cite specific evidence from the text to support your answer to question 3.**

   _____

   _____

   _____

STOP

© Frank Schaffer Publications

Asking and Responding to Open-Ended Questions

DIRECTIONS: Read the passage and then answer the questions on the next page.

Jackie Robinson

Jackie Robinson, born in 1919, was the first African-American man to play modern American major league baseball. In high school and college, he played many sports. He earned letters in track and field, basketball, football, and baseball. Unfortunately, Robinson had to quit college for financial reasons. It seemed his days of playing sports were over.

In 1942, Robinson was drafted into the army. He faced a lot of prejudice in the army. As an officer, he was asked to join the army football team. But when other teams objected to playing against a team with a black member, he turned to the army baseball team. There, he was rejected again because of his race.

After leaving the army in 1945, Robinson played shortstop for the Kansas City Monarchs, one of several teams in the Negro League. Professional baseball was still segregated at that time, but the Brooklyn Dodgers' president, Branch Rickey, recognized Robinson's athletic skills. Rickey was determined to make Robinson the first African-American player in major league baseball.

Robinson started playing with the Dodgers' farm team. Rickey advised Robinson not to fight back when people were unkind to him. Baseball players and fans alike thought he should not be allowed to play. He played so well, however, that in 1947, he joined the Brooklyn Dodgers.

At first, his teammates didn't like playing with him; however, when other people screamed at him, they came to his defense. Because of his great performance at second base and his outstanding batting average, Robinson was selected Rookie of the Year. In 1949, he was named the Most Valuable Player in the National League. One of his greatest thrills was when he helped the Dodgers win the 1955 World Series.

Jackie Robinson paved the way for African-American men to play in the major leagues. In 1962, he was inducted into baseball's Hall of Fame. Ten years later, at the age of 53, Robinson died in Stamford, Connecticut.

GO

© Frank Schaffer Publications

1. **How do you think Jackie Robinson felt toward Branch Rickey?**

_____

_____

_____

_____

_____

_____

_____

_____

2. **What effect did segregation have on professional baseball?**

_____

_____

_____

_____

_____

_____

_____

_____

3. **How do you think Robinson felt about his accomplishments?**

_____

_____

_____

_____

_____

_____

_____

_____

DIRECTIONS: Write two more questions that come to your mind after reading this story. The questions should be open-ended—not answered by a simple yes or no.

_____

_____

_____

_____

_____

_____

_____

_____

_____

_____

_____

_____

_____

_____

_____

_____

STOP

Comparing Similar Selections

DIRECTIONS: Read the following two poems. Then read the sentences below. Write the letter **A** if the sentence applies to the first poem. Write the letter **B** if the sentence applies to the second poem. Write a **C** if it applies to both poems. Write a **D** if it applies to neither poem.

Clue

A **limerick** is a humorous poem with five lines. The first, second, and fifth lines rhyme. A **quatrain** is a four-line poem with a set rhyme scheme.

Snow Day

A. The children awoke to a happy
            sight.
       While they were sleeping, the
            world had turned white.
       Their mother peered into their
            room and said,
       "No school today. Go back to
            bed!"

B. Father heard the news from his
            bed.
       He pulled the pillow over his head.
       Slipping on ice
       Is not very nice!
       He wished it were summer
            instead.

1. **This poem is a limerick.** _____

2. **This poem is a quatrain.** _____

3. **The person is annoyed.** _____

4. **Someone wants to go back to sleep.** _____

5. **Winter is welcomed.** _____

6. **The setting is winter.** _____

7. **The poem takes place at midnight.** _____

8. **The main idea of the poem is snow.** _____

9. **The main idea of the poem is a reaction to snow.** _____

10. **The person in the poem will have to to get up soon.** _____

11. **The people in the poem can go back to sleep for as long as they like.** _____

12. **The poem mentions an item from a bedroom.** _____

STOP

© Frank Schaffer Publications

Name _____ Date _____

Making Connections Through Analysis

DIRECTIONS: Read the passage and then answer the questions on the next page.

The Ship of the Desert

Nomads who crisscross the Sahara Desert of North Africa rely on a most unique animal for transportation—the dromedary, or one-humped camel. Because it is indispensable to desert travel, the dromedary is sometimes called the "ship of the desert."

Several factors make the dromedary suitable for long desert trips. It can go for long periods without nourishment. The hump on a camel's back serves as its food reserve. When it has little to eat, it converts the fat from its hump into energy. The camel's hump can weigh up to 80 pounds or more. When the animal has to rely on its reservoir of fat, the hump becomes much smaller. Thus, it is easy to recognize a well-fed camel by the size of its hump.

Many people believe that camels store water in their humps. This is not true. Their ability to go for days without drinking is due to other factors. First, camels are able to drink large quantities of water at one time. Some have been known to gulp 53 gallons in one day. Second, the camel sweats very little and can tolerate greater body temperatures. Consequently, it retains most of the water it drinks and can travel several hundred miles before replenishing its supply.

Other physical characteristics enable the camel to endure harsh desert conditions. It can completely close its nostrils, thus protecting it from the stinging effects of sandstorms. Its eyes are shielded from sand and sun by overhanging lids and long lashes, and its broad, padded feet keep it from sinking into the soft sand. No other animal is better equipped for life in the desert than the camel.

GO

© Frank Schaffer Publications

1. **What is the main idea expressed in this story?**

   (A) The dromedary is the ideal animal for desert life.

   (B) The camel's hump serves as its food reservoir.

   (C) The dromedary is called the "ship of the desert."

   (D) Camels do not store water in their humps.

2. **Which characteristic does not help the camel to survive in the desert?**

   (F) A camel can drink up to 53 gallons of water in one day.

   (G) A camel can close its nostrils.

   (H) A camel sweats very little.

   (J) A camel is indispensable to desert travel.

3. **What cannot be concluded from reading this passage?**

   (A) A camel can survive a long time without eating.

   (B) A dromedary camel is easier to ride than a Bactrian camel.

   (C) Camels have many features that equip them for cold weather.

   (D) Both B and C

4. **Which of these statements is not a fact stated in the passage?**

   (F) The hump is where the camel's food reserve is stored.

   (G) As a camel drinks more water, its hump becomes larger.

   (H) When a camel has little to eat, it converts the fat from the hump into energy.

   (J) You can recognize a well-fed camel by the size of its hump.

5. **Which of these statements is a fact?**

   (A) Nomads prefer camels to all other pack animals.

   (B) The Bactrian camel is the best camel for desert travel.

   (C) A camel's broad, padded feet protect it from sinking in soft sand.

   (D) Camels enjoy hot weather.

6. **Which additional detail would support the title of this story?**

   (F) Nomads use camel's hair to weave cloth to make tents.

   (G) Camels are strong animals capable of carrying loads up to a thousand pounds.

   (H) Camel's milk and meat are often part of the nomad's diet.

   (J) Camels can be stubborn.

7. **What is the author's purpose for this passage?**

   (A) to entertain

   (B) to inform

   (C) to persuade

   (D) to sell a product

STOP

© Frank Schaffer Publications

Name _____ Date _____

Selecting Appropriate Reading Strategies

DIRECTIONS: For each of the following situations, briefly describe the reading strategy you would select based on your purpose. For example, if you were putting together a model airplane, you would probably read the instructions closely; you would not skim the instructions or simply look for important key words.

1. **You want to find out what is on television Friday night at 8:00.**

   _____

   _____

   _____

   _____

   _____

2. **You want to find out if a reference book you are holding contains any information about spiders.**

   _____

   _____

   _____

   _____

   _____

3. **You are baking your first cake.**

   _____

   _____

   _____

   _____

   _____

4. **You want to learn about the life of John F. Kennedy.**

   _____

   _____

   _____

   _____

   _____

   _____

   _____

   _____

5. **You want to compare the rules of American and Canadian football.**

   _____

   _____

   _____

   _____

   _____

   _____

   _____

   _____

STOP

Reader Response and Interpretation

DIRECTIONS: Read the following story and then answer the questions on the next page.

The Rookie

It was like a dream come true. All through high school Bill had worked on his brother's stock cars hoping that someday he would be allowed to drive in a real race. For years he helped the maintenance crew water and pack the track. Finally, his patience paid off! As an eighteen-year-old senior, he would be the youngest driver ever to race on a popular, new dirt track.

Finally, the green flag came down, and the race was officially underway. During the first couple of laps, Bill carefully felt his way around the track, intent on maintaining his position. Feeling increasingly confident, he passed another car, this time on the inside of the track. "Wow!" he thought. "I really can do this!" But even before this thought had time to clear his mind, the car ahead of him lost a right, rear wheel. Taking a deep breath, Bill muttered to himself, "Phew! What will happen next?"

The red flag came out, and the tow truck removed the disabled car from the track. The racing officials lined up the cars for a restart. Bill found he had moved up three places. Confidently, Bill stepped on it at just the right moment. Dirt flew and engines roared as the drivers challenged each other for position. With only five laps left in the race, Bill was now in fourth place. He did not see the huge hole going into turn two, and he hit it at full speed! The car bounced up on two wheels and headed straight for a light pole at the track's edge. The force of the crash caused the windshield to pop out, just as Bill's head snapped forward. So much for "I can do it!" Bill thought, as he regained his senses.

Bill graduated from high school with a broken nose, two black eyes, and a swollen lip, twice its normal size. Bill had learned some valuable lessons from his first night of racing. First, he learned to make sure his seat belt was tightly fastened. Bill was also able to verify what he already knew; racing was in his blood.

GO

© Frank Schaffer Publications

Name _____ Date _____

DIRECTIONS: Answer the questions by filling in your answers next to the headings, "Your response." Then find a friend or family member whose feelings toward motor racing are completely different from yours. (If you love it, for example, find someone who dislikes it.) Have that person fill in his or her answers to the questions by the headings, "Friend's response." Then compare the answers.

1. **What is the main idea of this story?**

   Your response: _____

   _____

   _____

   _____

   Friend's response: _____

   _____

   _____

   _____

2. **Describe Bill's character and personality.**

   Your response: _____

   _____

   _____

   _____

   Friend's response: _____

   _____

   _____

   _____

3. **What do you think Bill should do after graduation?**

   Your response: _____

   _____

   _____

   _____

   Friend's response: _____

   _____

   _____

   _____

4. **What is your impression of the sport of motor racing after reading this story?**

   Your response: _____

   _____

   _____

   _____

   Friend's response: _____

   _____

   _____

   _____

STOP

Identifying the Author's Purpose

DIRECTIONS: Read the passage and then answer the questions on the next page.

Paws With a Cause

Paws With a Cause (PAWS) is a nonprofit organization that provides specially trained "hearing" and "service" dogs to people with disabilities. It began in 1979 in Byron Center, Michigan, and was originally called Ears for the Deaf.

At first, the organization trained dogs to assist the hearing impaired. Over time, they expanded their service to training "service" dogs. A service dog allows a physically challenged person to have more independence. In addition, PAWS trains dogs to help individuals with multiple handicaps.

PAWS trainers select dogs from animal shelters and humane societies across the United States. Over 95 percent of the hearing dogs have been saved from possible death at these shelters. These dogs are then taken to the training center, where they spend several months in specific skill training.

The dogs' training consists of three parts. All the dogs are given basic obedience training. They learn to respond to commands such as "sit," "come," and "down." Dogs being trained for the hearing impaired are also given specific sound-alert training. These dogs learn to respond to six sounds: door knock, doorbell ring, two types of telephone rings, alarm clock, smoke alarm, and an intruder. Service dogs receive advanced training geared to the individual person's needs. They may learn how to turn off lights, pick up dropped objects, close doors, or serve as a support for walking. The third phase of training takes place at the recipient's home. A field trainer helps the dog bond with a new owner, learn commands, and get familiar with the needs and routines of the owner.

A trained dog is expensive. A hearing dog costs approximately $5,000. A service dog costs around $8,500. Individuals with disabilities may purchase the dogs with their own money. PAWS has an active donation fund to assist individuals with the expenses incurred, but the waiting period is lengthy. Some organizations sponsor walk-a-thons or other fund drives to raise money for a member of their community. Also, generous students have earned money through creative methods such as the Read-a-Million-Minutes program.

In addition to rescuing many dogs from animal shelters and then training them for specific service, PAWS spends a great deal of time educating the public. Through community awareness presentations, PAWS is helping the public understand the legal rights of dogs for the hearing impaired and service dogs and the need for these dogs. With the help of these dogs, having a disability does not mean living with an inability.

© Frank Schaffer Publications

Name _____ Date _____

DIRECTIONS: One way the author demonstrates a purpose for writing is in the information he or she chooses to include. Complete the story map with details from the passage.

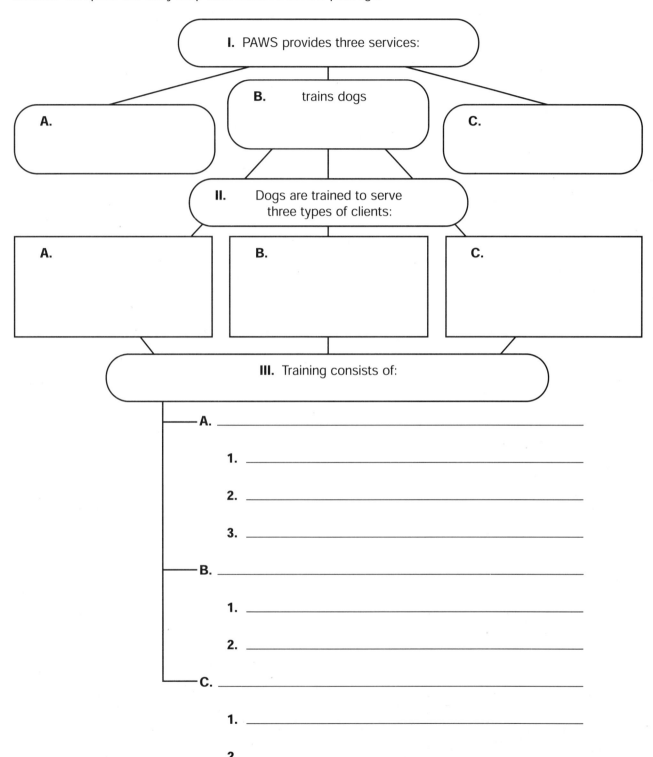

I. PAWS provides three services:

A.

B.   trains dogs

C.

II.   Dogs are trained to serve three types of clients:

A.

B.

C.

III. Training consists of:

A. _____

    1. _____

    2. _____

    3. _____

B. _____

    1. _____

    2. _____

C. _____

    1. _____

    2. _____

IV. Write a sentence summarizing the author's purpose in giving these details in *Paws With a Cause.*

_____

_____

STOP

© Frank Schaffer Publications

Reading

1C.9

Interpreting Imagery and Figurative Language

DIRECTIONS: Read the poems by Carl Sandburg and answer the questions.

Fog
The fog comes
in on little cat feet.

It sits looking
over harbor and city
on silent haunches
and then moves on.

Grass
Pile the bodies high at Austerlitz and Waterloo.
Shovel them under and let me work—
    I am the grass; I cover all.

And pile them high at Gettysburg
And pile them high at Ypres and Verdun.
Shovel them under and let me work.
Two years, ten years, and passengers ask the conductor:
    What place is this?
    Where are we now?

    I am the grass.
    Let me work.

Note: The poem cites famous battlefields of the Napoleonic Wars, American Civil War, and World War I.

Sources: "Fog," by Carl Sandburg, from *Anthology of American Literature, Volume 2: Realism to the Present,* New York: Macmillan, 1980, p. 1017. "Grass," by Carl Sandburg, from *Anthology of American Literature, Volume 2: Realism to the Present,* New York: Macmillan, 1980, p. 1018.

1. **Which type of figurative device is used in the poem *Fog*?**

   Ⓐ onomatopoeia

   Ⓑ metaphor

   Ⓒ idiom

   Ⓓ analogy

2. **Describe the use of personification in one of the poems.**

   _____

   _____

   _____

3. **What is fog compared to in the first poem? Do you think this is an appropriate or inappropriate comparison?**

   _____

   _____

   _____

4. **In which poem is the imagery easier to understand? Explain your answer.**

   _____

   _____

   _____

© Frank Schaffer Publications

Name _____ Date _____

Reading

1C.10

Read with
Understanding
and Fluency

Expressing Ideas
in Illustrations

DIRECTIONS: Examine and think about the illustration below and answer the questions that follow.

1. What *ideas* are being expressed in the illustration? Answer as completely as you can.

   _____
   _____
   _____
   _____
   _____
   _____
   _____
   _____
   _____

2. What do you think the illustrator's *feelings* were as he drew this image? How can you tell?

   _____
   _____
   _____
   _____
   _____
   _____
   _____
   _____
   _____

Source: Downloaded from http://mackaycartoons.net/september11.html
on the World Wide Web on 10/15/03.

Reading

| 1C.12 |

Recognizing Media's Influence on Fiction

DIRECTIONS: Read the following book review and tell how it might influence whether or not you decide to read the book. Explain your answer.

Michael's Latest a Bore

Marie Michael's latest volume in her King Titan series, *The Return of Titan*, is a real letdown. The title character, the exiled King Titan, seems to have undergone a personality change since the last installment, *Titan in a Tempest*. The once-interesting, complex character has been transformed into a boring, paint-by-numbers stick figure, spouting lines such as, "You haven't seen the last of me!" and plotting ridiculous revenge on his enemies. Even the secondary characters, like the humorous Polly and the romantic duo of Fosworth and Delight, can't breath life into this tired plot. Perhaps it's finally time for Michael to remove King Titan's crown once and for all and move on to another subject.

1. _____

_____

_____

_____

_____

_____

DIRECTIONS: Write a brief review of the book you most recently read. Show the review to a friend or family member. How did your review influence the person's desire to read the book?

2. _____

_____

_____

_____

_____

_____

_____

_____

_____

_____

_____

_____

_____

_____

_____

_____

DIRECTIONS: Find and save a book review from a newspaper or a magazine. Read just enough of the review to get the name of the book, then obtain the book from the library and read it yourself. Then read the book review. Answer the following questions on a separate sheet of paper: How did the reviewer's view differ from your own? Had you read the review before reading the book, would your feeling toward the book have changed? Why or why not?

STOP

© Frank Schaffer Publications

1C.13

Applying Appropriate Reading Strategies

DIRECTIONS: Read the passages and answer the questions on the next page.

A
Rose, harsh rose,
marred and with stint of petals,
meager flower thin, sparse of leaf,
more precious
than a wet rose
single on a stem—
you are caught in the drift.

B
Born in 1888, Huddie Ledbetter,
nicknamed "Leadbelly," was a blues
guitarist who inspired generations of
musicians. For much of his life, he
wandered from place to place, playing
anywhere he could. In 1934, he was
discovered by John and Alan Lomax,
who helped him find a larger audience
for his music. Soon he was playing in
colleges, clubs, and music halls. He
was featured on radio and television
shows. Leadbelly died in 1949, but his
music lives on. Musicians in every style
credit him with laying the foundation
for today's popular music.

C
Frivolous lawsuits have repeatedly
been in the news. The family of
Giovanni A. Almovodar, New Jersey
prison inmate, filed a lawsuit against
the Camden County jail. The inmate
was 18 and awaiting trial on a murder
charge. He died when he fell on his
head during an escape attempt. The
family charged that the jailers did not
maintain a reasonably safe facility.

D
The grandmother didn't want to go to
Florida. She wanted to visit some of
her connections in east Tennessee and
she was seizing at every chance to
change Bailey's mind. Bailey was the
son she lived with, her only boy. He
was sitting on the edge of his chair at
the table, bent over the orange sports
section of the *Journal*. "Now look here,
Bailey," she said, "see here, read this,"
and she stood with one hand on her
thin hip and the other rattling the
newspaper at his bald head.

E
What triggers lightning? One theory
states that a bigger bit of ice slams
into a smaller bit of ice, leaving behind
a positive or negative charge. The
larger the bit of ice and the faster it is
going, the bigger the charge it leaves
behind. When enough of these charges
collect, lightning occurs.

F
COOK: Short-order cook needed at
Flynn's Diner. Shift: 12 midnight to 8
A.M. Must have reliable transportation
and references. Good pay and
benefits. Two free meals daily. Apply in
person at Flynn's Diner, 2000 Wharf
Street, near the harbor.

Sources: Selection A—from "Sea Rose," by H. D. [Hilda
Doolittle], from *The Norton Anthology of Poetry, Revised
Edition*, New York: Norton, 1975, p. 1009. Selection D—
from "A Good Man Is Hard to Find," by Flannery
O'Connor, from *Anthology of American Literature,
Volume 2: Realism to the Present*, New York: Macmillan,
1980, pp. 1739–1750.

GO

1. **Which of the following passages are nonfiction?**

   (A) passage B

   (B) passage C

   (C) passage E

   (D) All of the above

2. **Which passage requires you to pay particular attention to figurative language?**

   (F) passage A

   (G) passage B

   (H) passage E

   (J) passage F

3. **Which passage would you be more likely to read with an eye to literal truth?**

   (A) passage B

   (B) passage C

   (C) passage D

   (D) passage F

4. **Which passage could you more easily illustrate on a time line?**

   (F) passage A

   (G) passage B

   (H) passage E

   (J) passage F

5. **Which passage requires you to pay particular attention to a sequence of events?**

   (A) passage A

   (B) passage C

   (C) passage D

   (D) passage E

6. **What passage would you read to be entertained?**

   (F) passage B

   (G) passage C

   (H) passage D

   (J) passage E

7. **What passage would you read to be informed?**

   (A) passage B

   (B) passage C

   (C) passage E

   (D) All of the above

8. **What passage would you read to be informed?**

   (F) passage A

   (G) passage D

   (H) passage F

   (J) None of the above

STOP

© Frank Schaffer Publications

Name _____   Date _____

Reading

1.C

For pages 49–66

Mini-Test 3

Read with Understanding and Fluency

DIRECTIONS: Read the passage and then answer the questions on the next page.

The Stanley Cup

Today, one of the most popular spectator sports in the world is ice hockey. Each year, the teams of the National Hockey League play a series of games to determine who will win the championship of ice hockey. The winner is presented an award called the Stanley Cup. The Stanley Cup is one of the most prestigious awards in the world of sports.

Ice hockey is now an international sport. But nowhere is hockey more popular than in Canada. Over 125 years ago, hockey-on-ice was played in Montreal, Canada. In 1870, the first official rules of the game were written. By 1880, official teams were organized into leagues.

Some of the first league games were played on town ice rinks that had bandstands right in the middle of the rinks! Later, special ice hockey rinks were built that even featured lights hung from telegraph poles.

The popularity of the game seemed to sweep through Canada. One of hockey's greatest fans was Lord Stanley of Preston, the sixth Governor General of Canada. Lord Stanley organized a championship game in which Canadian ice hockey teams would compete.

On March 22, 1894, the first Stanley Cup game was played in Montreal, Canada, at Victoria Rink. The championship game received its name from the award presented to the winner. Donated by Lord Stanley, the first award was a sterling silver cup.

The original Stanley Cup has gone through several changes over the years. Bands were added on the bottom of the bowl to hold the names of more winners. After many years of wear, the original cup was retired to the Hockey Hall of Fame in 1969.

After that first championship game in 1894, the game of ice hockey continued

to grow in popularity. Today, the National Hockey League includes teams from America as well as Canada. The Montreal Canadiens hold the record for winning the most Stanley Cup championships. Each year, a new set of teams plays a series of games to determine who wins the championship of ice hockey and the Stanley Cup.

© Frank Schaffer Publications

1. **What was the author's purpose for writing this passage?**

    (A) To encourage the reader to like ice hockey as much as Canadians.

    (B) To explain the rules of ice hockey.

    (C) To entertain the reader with stories about ice hockey.

    (D) To inform the reader about the importance of the Stanley Cup.

2. **Which of these statements from the article supports the author's purpose for writing this passage?**

    (F) One of hockey's greatest fans was Lord Stanley of Preston.

    (G) The first Stanley Cup game was played in Montreal, Canada.

    (H) The Stanley Cup is one of the most prestigious awards in the world of sports.

    (J) The first official rules of the game were written.

3. **Which of the following is not an open-ended question?**

    (A) Why is the Stanley Cup so prestigious?

    (B) Do you like ice hockey?

    (C) How did ice hockey increase in popularity?

    (D) How is the National Hockey League organized?

DIRECTIONS: For each of the following situations, briefly describe the reading strategy you would select based on your purpose.

4. **You are preparing a time line of the major events in World War II.**

    (F) Read a biography of an important American general.

    (G) Scan an encyclopedia article about the war watching for dates and headings.

    (H) Carefully read a two-volume history of the war.

    (J) Read two articles about the war and create a Venn diagram comparing them.

5. **You are building an intricate model that has dozens of small pieces.**

    (A) Skim the directions.

    (B) Look for bold words in the directions.

    (C) Read directions carefully each step of the way.

    (D) Draw an outline of the directions.

DIRECTIONS: Read the passage below, then answer the questions.

As she walked along the sandy shore with delight at nature's wonders she did see starfish, whitecaps, conch shells, and more. She knew that she would never fly free like the tissue-paper seagulls above or swim with the dolphins she did love.

6. **What type of fiction is the passage above?**

    (F) novel

    (G) poem

    (H) play

    (J) folktale

7. **Which of the following is a metaphor?**

    (A) the sandy shore

    (B) tissue-paper seagulls

    (C) she would never fly free

    (D) nature's wonders

© Frank Schaffer Publications

Reading Standards

Read and Understand Literature

Goal 2: Read and understand literature representative of various societies, eras, and ideas.

Learning Standard 2A—Students who meet the standard can understand how literary elements and techniques are used to convey meaning.

1. Read a wide range of fiction.
2. Identify literary elements and literary techniques (e.g., satire, characterization, narration, dialogue, figurative language) in a variety of genres and tell how they affect the work. *(See page 70.)*
3. Predict how the story might be different if the author changed certain literary elements or techniques (e.g., dialect, setting, vocabulary). *(See pages 71–72.)*
4. Describe how the development of theme, character, plot, and setting contribute to the overall impact of a piece of literature. *(See page 73.)*
5. Compare selections with similar characters, plots, and/or themes. *(See pages 74–75.)*
6. Understand and use literary terms (e.g., foreshadowing, metaphor, simile, symbolism, flashback, scene, dialogue). *(See pages 76–77.)*

What it means:
- **Foreshadowing** is the use of clues by the author to prepare the reader for events that will happen in the story.
- **Symbolism** is the use of images to represent story ideas, for example, climbing a mountain can symbolize the process of resolving a problem.

7. Transfer new vocabulary from literature into other contexts. *(See page 78.)*
8. Identify characteristics and authors associated with various literary forms (e.g., short stories, novels, drama, fables, biographies, documentaries, poetry, science fiction). *(See pages 79–80.)*
9. Recognize and use cognitive strategies (e.g., analysis, synthesis, inference) to enhance understanding. *(See pages 81–82.)*
10. Compare ways in which different kinds of literature are organized (e.g., plays, short stories, essays, poems). *(See page 83.)*

Learning Standard 2B *(See page 86.)*

Name _____ Date _____

Identifying Literary Techniques in a Poem

DIRECTIONS: Read the poem and then answer the questions.

Whitesox

Sanding the board,
My cat, Whitesox.
Her tongue,
Like fine grains of sand
On paper,
Licking the wood.
An electric sander
Giving out a quiet purr.
Like a nail file,
Smoothing out the edges.

Ouch! A splinter.

 Clue Modern poets often write **free-verse poems.** As the term indicates, the poet is free from conventions; free-verse poems do not contain regular rhythm or rhyme. Although poets may take certain liberties with the language, they often use natural rhythms and figures of speech, which help free-verse poems maintain their form.

1. To what does the poet compare the cat's tongue?

   _____

   _____

2. What two things in the poem could be "giving out a quiet purr"?

   _____

   _____

3. Circle the periods in the poem. Does every line end with a period? What can you conclude about free-verse poems after seeing where the poet ends sentences?

   _____

   _____

4. What might the "splinter" be that Whitesox comes across in the process of cleaning herself?

   _____

   _____

5. Write a free-verse poem of your own about a pet.

   _____

   _____

   _____

   _____

   _____

   _____

STOP

© Frank Schaffer Publications

Name _____ Date _____

Reading

2A.3

Read and
Understand
Literature

Effect of Technique on a Story

DIRECTIONS: Read the story and then answer the questions on the next page.

Sleepwalking

ZzZzZzZzZz

"Dad? Do you have a minute to help me with my speech?" I asked after supper.

"Sure," said Dad. "I'd love to help."

Dad settles on the couch. I stand tall, grasp my note cards, and smile. "Be honest. I need a good grade," I say. He nods and I begin. "Ever fight falling asleep for seven hours straight?"

"Ever want control over your life?" I pause for effect. "If you answered yes, then you have something in common with me and all students."

"Nice opening," Dad says, and I smile.

"Students all over the United States are plagued with sleep deprivation. If schools really wanted students to learn better, they would begin school at 11 A.M. and end school at 2 P.M."

"That's a bit exaggerated," Dad says. I nod, stand up straight, glance quickly at my note cards and begin again. "Research shows the preteen brain needs 10 to 12 hours of sleep. Research suggests that children learn best after 10 A.M. Studies also indicate that attention spans are only 20 minutes long."

"Is that true?" Dad asks. "Sounds like you're twisting facts."

"Sort of," I say. I shuffle my cards and continue. "The trouble is that school starts at 7:30 A.M., which means most students are really sleepwalking. Nobody wakes up until lunchtime. Plus, if the attention span is only 20 minutes, it makes sense to change classes to 20 minutes each. Students would be more alert and would learn more. Therefore, I recommend a later start time and 20-minute classes." I smile.

"Well, what do you think?"

"I recommend you rethink the point of the speech."

"But what about my delivery?" I ask impatiently.

"Good voice and delivery, but your speech is not logical."

"I'm getting graded on speech skills and facts, not logic, Dad."

"Winona, rethink the speech." Dad uses his better-do-what-I-say voice.

I shuffle my note cards. I think, *Maybe he's right. I could add the facts about brain waves and learning to read or a list of the eight intelligences.*

I smile. "Okay, I'll add more facts."

1. **When a story is told in first person, a narrator tells a personal story from his or her point of view. Who is the narrator of this story?**

   _____

   _____

2. **What does Dad say makes Winona's speech good?**

   (A) It has good facts.

   (B) It has a good opening.

   (C) It has a good idea.

   (D) She has good delivery.

3. **What does Dad say makes Winona's speech weak?**

   (F) It twists facts and information.

   (G) It has a weak conclusion.

   (H) It is not logical.

   (J) She uses a weak voice.

4. **What does Dad suggest Winona do to improve her speech?**

   _____

   _____

   _____

   _____

   _____

   _____

5. **How might the story be different if another person narrated the story? Explain your answer with evidence from the story.**

   _____

   _____

   _____

   _____

   _____

   _____

   _____

   _____

   _____

   _____

   _____

   _____

   _____

   _____

   _____

   _____

   _____

   _____

   _____

   _____

STOP

© Frank Schaffer Publications

Reading

2A.4

Character Development

DIRECTIONS: Read the story and then fill in the character webs with words that describe the characters in the reading selection.

Save the Day

He greeted his teammates, jumping up and down. "Are you ready to win the championship?" he asked excitedly.

His two best friends, Jeffrey and Alyssa, smiled at his excitement. "It looks like our star batter is ready," Jeffrey said. Jeffrey didn't want to admit that he was pretty nervous. Lately, he'd been in a slump. His average had declined late in the season. He hoped he could pull it back up today when it counted most.

Alyssa was calm, as usual. She never seemed to get butterflies in her stomach, even under pressure. She was the team's pitcher and had a mean fastball.

The players warmed up and took the field. The game was a close one, but Tate and his team were victorious in the end. Afterward, the three buddies went to a nearby ice-cream shop to celebrate.

"Great job today, Alyssa!" Tate complimented his friend. "You kept your cool even when we were behind 2 to 0."

"Thanks." Alyssa said modestly. She licked her black raspberry cone neatly. Not a drip escaped off the cone.

"You were pretty great yourself," Jeffrey said to Tate. "I jumped off the bench, almost knocking it over, when you hit that ball over the fence in the fifth inning!" The two boys gave each other high fives. In their enthusiasm, the boys knocked Tate's ice cream off its cone.

"Oh, no," Tate said, disappointedly.

"Sorry, Tate," Jeffrey said. But Jeffrey couldn't stop smiling. He was in too good a mood. He'd hit the winning run today, and he felt great. He hadn't let his team down. Now, he wouldn't let his friend down.

"I have some money left," he said to Tate. "Let's go back up to the counter so I can save the day again!"

Tate

How he feels before the game _____

Why? _____

What he does during the game _____

_____

What he probably does next _____

_____

Jeffrey

How he feels before the game _____

Why? _____

What he does during the game _____

_____

What he probably does next _____

_____

Alyssa

How she feels before the game _____

Why? _____

What she does during the game _____

What she probably does next _____

STOP

© Frank Schaffer Publications

Reading

2A.5

Comparing
Similar Selections

DIRECTIONS: Read the stories and then answer the questions on the next page.

What Do You Wanna Play?

"What do you wanna play?" Will asked as he shoved a bite of pancake into his mouth.

"Scramble. We are Scramble maniacs at this house," said Scott.

Will poured more orange juice into his glass. "How about that game where you ask dumb questions about stuff everyone always forgets?"

"Trivial Questions," said Scott.

"Yeah, that's it."

"Can you name the seven dwarfs?" asked Eric.

"Snoopy, Sneezy, Dopey," said Scott.

"Nah, Snoopy's a dog," said Eric.

"Let's do something else," Will chimed in as he cut his pancake in half.

"Let's play Scramble," said Scott.

"That's too much like school. Let's play football," said Eric.

"It's too cold out," said Scott.

"Let's dig out your connector sets. I haven't played with those for years," Eric said as he pushed his chair back and stood.

"Yeah," said Scott and Will as they jumped from their seats.

Corrals in the Heavens

The spirited orange, yellow, and red flames reached upward toward the starry sky from the crackling campfire. It was nearly midnight. Cathy and Stacey were sprawled out around the campfire, carefully roasting the remaining marshmallows to a perfect bubbly brown. The girls resisted the need to end a perfect day.

Cathy and Stacy had been best friends since first grade. During their summer vacations, they were particularly attracted to horse-related activities. Cathy and Stacey had received their horses on the same Christmas four years earlier.

Now that Cathy and Stacey were in sixth grade, their parents knew they were responsible enough for trail-riding and camping together. Stacey's dad had made arrangements to borrow a double horse trailer to transport the horses to Loud Thunder Forest Preserve. The horses quickly greeted each other as friends in this long-awaited rendezvous.

"Look at that Big Dipper!" Cathy's father noticed as he pointed up to the late evening sky. "It looks like it's pouring a drink for your horses."

"There we are, Stacey," whispered Cathy, pointing to the stars. "We're riding our horses on that star next to the Big Dipper. We better be cautious of that Great Bear and her Little Bear cub."

"Let's leap to that neighboring bright star to avoid spooking the horses," added Stacey, quickly joining the inventive fantasy game.

The girls continued their journey, each trying to out-best the other with her fantasy. Together they rode their horses from one constellation to another, escaping lions and bears.

Finally, the girls exhausted the game and the campsite became quiet. They couldn't resist their heavy, drooping eyelids and finally agreed to enter the tent for the night. They knew that early morning would bring a real-life riding adventure.

74

© Frank Schaffer Publications

1. **What is the setting for the story, "What Do You Wanna Play?"**

   (A) Scott's bedroom

   (B) Scott's living room

   (C) Scott's kitchen

   (D) Scott's basement

2. **What is the setting for the story, "Corrals in the Heavens"?**

   (F) riding on a trail

   (G) sitting around a campfire

   (H) camping in a state park

   (J) eating in a kitchen

3. **What theme do both of these stories have in common?**

   _____

   _____

   _____

   _____

   _____

   _____

   _____

   _____

4. **How are the characters in these stories alike?**

   _____

   _____

   _____

   _____

   _____

   _____

   _____

   _____

_____

_____

_____

_____

_____

5. **Identify some differences between Cathy and Stacey and Will and Scott.**

   _____

   _____

   _____

   _____

   _____

   _____

   _____

   _____

   _____

   _____

   _____

   _____

   _____

   _____

   _____

   _____

   _____

STOP

Understanding and Using Literary Terms

DIRECTIONS: Read the poem.

Black-Eyed Rebel

A poem by Will Carleton

A boy drove into the city, his wagon
  loaded down
With food to feed the people of the
  British-governed town;
And the little black-eyed rebel, so
  innocent and sly,
Was watching for his coming from the
  corner of her eye. . . .

He drove up to the market, he waited in
  the line;
His apples and potatoes were fresh and
  fair and fine;
But long and long he waited, and no one
  came to buy,
Save the black-eyed rebel, watching
  from the corner of her eye.

"Now who will buy my apples?" he
  shouted, long and loud;
And "Who wants my potatoes?" he
  repeated to the crowd;
But from all the people round him came
  no word of reply,
Save the black-eyed rebel, answering
  from the corner of her eye.

For she knew that 'neath the lining of the
  coat he wore that day,
Were long letters from the husbands and
  the fathers far away,
Who were fighting for the freedom that
  they meant to gain or die;
And a tear like silver glistened in the
  corner of her eye.

But the treasures—how to get them?
  crept the questions through her
  mind,
Since keen enemies were watching for
  what prizes they might find;
And she paused a while and pondered,
  with a pretty little sigh;
Then resolve crept through her features,
  and a shrewdness fired her eye.

So she resolutely walked up to the
  wagon old and red;
"May I have a dozen apples for a kiss?"
  she sweetly said:
And the brown face flushed to scarlet;
  for the boy was somewhat shy,
And he saw her laughing at him from the
  corner of her eye. . . .

Clinging round his brawny neck, she
  clasped her fingers white and small,
And then whispered, "Quick! the letters!
  thrust them underneath my shawl!
Carry back again this package, and be
  sure that you are spry!"
And she sweetly smiled upon him from
  the corner of her eye. . . .

With the news of loved ones absent to
  the dear friends they would greet,
Searching them who hungered for them,
  swift she glided through the street.
"There is nothing worth the doing
  that it does not pay to try,"
Thought the little black-eyed rebel,
  with a twinkle in her eye.

GO

© Frank Schaffer Publications

Name _____ Date _____

DIRECTIONS: Several literary terms are listed below. Identify and describe them using the poem on page 76.

Clue

The heroine's name was Mary Redmond, and she lived in Philadelphia. During the occupation of that town by the British, she was ever ready to aid in the secret delivery of the letters written home by the husbands and fathers fighting in the Continental Army.

Setting

_____
_____

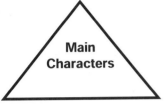

Main Characters

_____
_____

Plot

Problem: _____
_____

Goal: _____
_____

Episodes

_____
_____

Climax

_____
_____

Resolution

_____
_____

STOP

© Frank Schaffer Publications

Using New Vocabulary

DIRECTIONS: Read the story and pay particular attention to the underlined words. Then write a new story of your own, using each of the underlined words in the story. Write the story below and use an extra sheet of paper, if needed. Consult a dictionary for the meaning of the words if you are unsure about them.

A Country Night

Gazing out my bedroom window at stars I never knew existed, I saw rainbow-colored lights flash across the ink-black sky. The lights seemed to twist and twirl like a <u>kaleidoscope</u>. Surprisingly, they <u>spiraled</u> down just beyond the barn in a clump of trees. Being as curious as the cat that prowled outside my bedroom window, I decided to investigate.

I threw on my clothes, crawled out the window, and tramped through what I hoped was mud in the barnyard. Cautiously I peered out from behind a tree. Three <u>translucent</u> and completely hairless creatures were glaring back at me! I was frozen and speechless. The creatures spoke in what seemed like a variety of strange languages, while <u>manipulating</u> control panels on their belts. Suddenly, their words sounded familiar. My face must have lit up, because they made a final adjustment on their belts and spoke in clear English to me. "What is your name?" I told them my name was Aaron.

They were pretty friendly. The aliens' ship had broken down. Their flight into the galaxy had been <u>turbulent</u>, and some instrument cables had become loosened and <u>frayed</u>. We were all questioning my ability to find some extra parts and repair the damage. I finally accepted the challenge. After all, what else could I do?

Although my uncle's workshop in the back of the barn had enough materials to stock a machine repair shop, it lacked neatness. The aliens' flashlight-like eyes soon <u>spied</u> some promising cables that we took back to their spaceship. After hours of trial, and many trips back and forth to the barn, their spacecraft was ready for lift-off. They asked me to travel through space with them. I considered this unlikely escape from Clarksville and <u>reluctantly</u> declined their invitation. I was beginning to like it here. Before flying off, they gave me a prism as a gift of appreciation.

_____

_____

_____

_____

_____

_____

_____

_____

_____

_____

_____

STOP

© Frank Schaffer Publications

Reading
2A.8

Identifying Forms of Fiction

DIRECTIONS: Based on the passages below, identify the form of fiction of each.

1. **Act IV**

    Timothy enters his apartment and finds the furniture overturned, things thrown from the drawers. He picks up the telephone and dials 9-1-1.

    TIMOTHY: (fearfully) Yes, I need to report a break-in! (pause) No, I haven't searched the entire apartment. (pause) Do you really think they could still be here?!

    _____

2. **Starry night, Starry night**
    Twinkling dots of distant light.

    Constellations twirl around
    While I sit watching on the ground!

    _____

3. **Raccoon sat on the beach eating his potato. Before each bite he dipped the potato into the water. Monkey watched him from his perch in the tree and wondered about this curious habit.**

    _____

4. **The Himalayas are sometimes called the tallest mountains on earth. The truth is that several underwater ranges are even higher.**

    A passage like this would most likely be found in a book of _____ .

    - (A) fables
    - (B) facts
    - (C) tall tales
    - (D) adventure stories

DIRECTIONS: Based on the titles below, identify the form of fiction of each.

5. *King Arthur and the Blazing Sword*
    - (F) novel
    - (G) play
    - (H) legend
    - (J) folktale

6. *Adventure to Venus*
    - (A) novel
    - (B) play
    - (C) legend
    - (D) folktale

7. "Ode to an Owl, the Wisest of Fowl"
    - (F) play
    - (G) legend
    - (H) novel
    - (J) poetry

8. *How the Zebra Got His Stripes*
    - (A) legend
    - (B) folktale
    - (C) poetry
    - (D) novel

GO

Name _____ Date _____

DIRECTIONS: The following list tells you about four types of stories, called *genres*. Read each story below and write the kind of story it is on the line.

Science Fiction   a make-believe story based on scientific possibilities. Science fiction is also called fantasy, but it can include scientific facts.

Myth   a make-believe story that explains how something came to be. Myths often describe how the world was created.

Nonfiction   factual information. Nonfiction stories are true.

Realistic Fiction   a make-believe story that could actually happen. These stories aren't true, but it's easy to believe they are.

Juniper trees grow in Arizona. Tiny fairies live in their trunks. During the full moon, the fairies come out and dance at night. While dancing, they place blue berries on each tree for decoration. That's how the juniper gets its berries.

9. _____

"It's a bird!" Tim shouted. "It's a plane!" Connie said. But it was a spaceship! It landed next to a juniper tree. Little green men got off the spaceship. They clipped off several branches of the tree. "They're collecting tree samples to study on Mars," Connie whispered. They watched amazed as the spaceship disappeared into the sky.

10. _____

Jason and Patrick went for a hike. Because they were in the high desert, they carried water with them. When they got tired, the two boys sat in the shade of a juniper tree to rest and drink their water. That's when the rattlesnake appeared. "Don't move!" Patrick said to Jason. The boys sat still until the snake moved away. "What an adventure!" Jason said as the two boys returned home.

11. _____

Juniper trees are small, gnarly trees that grow in many parts of the world. Members of the evergreen family, they remain green year round. Juniper trees can be easily identified by their tiny blue or red berries. There are 13 different kinds of juniper trees in the United States. One kind of juniper tree is called the alligator juniper because its bark looks similar to the skin of an alligator. It grows in the Southwest.

12. _____

© Frank Schaffer Publications

Using Cognitive Strategies to Enhance Understanding

DIRECTIONS: Read the story and then answer the questions on the next page.

A Handful of Pretty Flowers

When Shanda first arrived at school, she discovered to her dismay that a freckle-faced boy in her sixth grade class was smitten with her. Because Shanda's family was new to the city, Shanda had not yet made any friends. She didn't feel comfortable asking the other students the boy's name. And he didn't offer his name, just a handful of pretty flowers.

Shanda soon learned the redheaded boy's name, Tommy. Whenever the class lined up for assembly or gym, he always smiled a crooked smile in her direction. Shanda felt uncomfortable with the attention he gave her, small though it was. Why did he like her anyway? On several occasions, Shanda tried to start a conversation with Tommy. But he always blushed, put his hands in his pockets, and looked down in embarrassment.

Gradually, Shanda developed a circle of friends. She finally felt happy in her new school. The only thing that still made her uncomfortable was Tommy with his crooked, shy smiles.

One day, as Shanda was walking down the hallway, Tommy came up alongside her. "Do you like animals?" he asked. Shanda was shocked. He had actually spoken to her.

Shanda turned to him and replied, "Hi, Tommy. Yeah, I like animals. We have lots of pets at my house. How about you?"

Shanda noticed how nervous Tommy had become as she talked. He even appeared to stop breathing for a moment. He whispered something about a dog and then hurried away. Shanda wondered if she had hurt his feelings by calling him Tommy. Maybe he liked to be called Tom.

A week later, Tommy reverently handed Shanda a photo. It was a snapshot of a beautiful collie. She had intelligent eyes and almost seemed to be smiling. Her ears were alert, and her face tilted questioningly. Shanda knew this was an important moment for Tommy. "What's her name?" she asked softly.

"Sh-, sh-, she was Shanda . . . like you. We had her since I was in kindergarten. Sh-, she's gone now."

© Frank Schaffer Publications

1. **What is this story mainly about?**

   Ⓐ a girl has a hard time fitting in at a new school

   Ⓑ a boy's love for his dog

   Ⓒ a shy boy

   Ⓓ a new girl at school and the shy boy who likes her

2. **In this story, what does the word *smitten* mean?**

   Ⓕ struck by

   Ⓖ attacked by

   Ⓗ attracted to

   Ⓙ bothered by

3. **From reading this story, we can conclude that**

   Ⓐ Tommy's dog has died, and he misses her.

   Ⓑ Tommy's family now has a cat.

   Ⓒ Tommy likes the name Shanda.

   Ⓓ Tommy thinks Shanda is cute.

4. **What probably caused Tommy to give Shanda flowers?**

   Ⓕ He felt sorry for her because she was a new girl.

   Ⓖ She and his dog shared the name Shanda.

   Ⓗ She had hair the same color as his collie.

   Ⓙ She liked animals as much as he did.

5. **From whose point of view is this story told?**

   Ⓐ Tommy's

   Ⓑ Shanda's

   Ⓒ the teacher's

   Ⓓ Shanda's friend

6. **Which statement best describes Shanda?**

   Ⓕ Shanda is popular.

   Ⓖ Shanda likes Tommy.

   Ⓗ Shanda shows kindness by asking about Tommy's dog.

   Ⓙ Shanda is shy.

STOP

© Frank Schaffer Publications

Reading

2A.10

Read and
Understand
Literature

Organization of Various Literary Genres

DIRECTIONS: Choose the best answer.

1. **Which of the following is most likely to be organized into *stanzas*?**
   - (A) biography
   - (B) essay
   - (C) poem
   - (D) novel

2. **Which of the following is most likely to be organized into *chapters*?**
   - (F) novel
   - (G) play
   - (H) short story
   - (J) poem

3. **Which of the following is most likely to have *scenes*?**
   - (A) short story
   - (B) folktale
   - (C) play
   - (D) poem

4. **Which of the following is most likely to be organized in *chronological order*?**
   - (F) fantasy tale
   - (G) mystery
   - (H) biography
   - (J) satire

5. **Which of the following is most likely to be organized into *acts*?**
   - (A) short story
   - (B) folktale
   - (C) play
   - (D) poem

6. **Which of the following is most likely to include a *moral* at the end?**
   - (F) biography
   - (G) documentary
   - (H) fable
   - (J) essay

7. **Which of the following is most likely to have line numbers?**
   - (A) biography
   - (B) essay
   - (C) novel
   - (D) poem

STOP

Name _____ Date _____

Reading

2A

For pages 70–83

Read and
Understand
Literature

Mini-Test 4

DIRECTIONS: Read the story and then answer the questions on the next page.

A New Tipi

Fingers of frost tickled at Little Deer's feet. It was a chilly fall morning, but there was no time for Little Deer to snuggle beneath her buffalo skins. It was going to be a busy day, helping her mother to finish the cover for their family's new tipi.

Little Deer slid her tunic over her head and fastened her moccasins. Wrapping herself up in another skin, she walked outside to survey the work they had done so far. The tipi cover was beautiful and nearly complete. The vast semicircle was spread across the ground, a patchwork in various shades of brown. After her father and brothers had killed the buffalo, she and her mother had carefully cured and prepared the skins, stretching them and scraping them until they were buttery soft. Then with needles made from bone and thread made from animal sinew, they had carefully sewn the hides together until they formed a huge canvas nearly thirty feet across.

After they finished the cover today, it would be ready to mount on the lodge poles. Little Deer's father had traded with another tribe for fourteen tall, wooden poles. They would stack the poles together in a cone shape, lashing them together with more rope made from animal sinews.

Then they would carefully stretch the cover over the poles, forming a snug, watertight home. Little Deer smiled in anticipation. She could just imagine the cozy glow of the fire through the tipi walls at night.

84

© Frank Schaffer Publications

1. **What is this story mainly about?**

   (A) hunting

   (B) building a tipi

   (C) the uses of buffalo

   (D) the life of a Native American girl

2. **Which sentence below is not a step in the process of making a tipi?**

   (F) Stretch the cover over the poles.

   (G) Cure and prepare the skins.

   (H) Sew the hides together.

   (J) Make clothing from the remaining pieces of hide.

3. **How does Little Deer feel about finishing the tipi?**

   (A) depressed

   (B) angry

   (C) excited

   (D) cold

4. **What does the term <u>sinew</u> mean in this passage?**

   (F) hair

   (G) skin

   (H) tendon

   (J) patchwork

5. **Which of these statements shows personification?**

   (A) Little Deer smiled in anticipation.

   (B) Little Deer slid her tunic over her head and fastened her moccasins.

   (C) The tipi cover was beautiful and nearly complete.

   (D) Fingers of frost tickled at Little Deer's feet.

6. **Where would this passage most likely be found?**

   (F) a historical novel

   (G) an encyclopedia

   (H) a science fiction story

   (J) a diary

7. **Which characteristic most accurately describes Little Deer?**

   (A) lazy

   (B) hardworking

   (C) clever

   (D) intelligent

8. **Suppose the author had set the story in modern-day America. In what ways might the story have been different? Be specific.**

   _____

   _____

   _____

   _____

   _____

   _____

   _____

   _____

   _____

   _____

   _____

   _____

   _____

STOP

Reading Standards

Read and Understand Literature

Goal 2: Read and understand literature representative of various societies, eras, and ideas.

Learning Standard 2A *(See page 69.)*

Learning Standard 2B—Students who meet the standard can read and interpret a variety of literary works.

1. Respond to fiction using interpretive and evaluative processes. *(See pages 87–88.)*
2. Select favorite authors and genres. *(See page 89.)*
3. Connect literary selections to historical context. *(See page 90.)*
4. Make inferences, draw conclusions, and make connections from text to text, text to self, and text to world. *(See pages 91–92.)*
5. Discuss recurring themes across works in print and media. *(See page 93.)*
6. Compare themes, conflicts, and figurative language from diverse times and cultures. *(See page 94.)*
7. Make inferences and draw conclusions about contexts, events, character, and settings. *(See pages 95–96.)*
8. Discuss the impact of author's word choice on content. *(See page 97.)*
9. Interpret nonfiction text and informational materials.
10. Support plausible interpretations with evidence from the text. *(See pages 98–99.)*

© Frank Schaffer Publications

2B.1

Interpreting and Evaluating Literature

DIRECTIONS: Use your interpretive skills to match each of the qualities on the left with the quotation on the right. Write the letter in the proper blank.

1. _____ **hot-tempered**

2. _____ **embarrassed**

3. _____ **confused**

4. _____ **tired**

5. _____ **sneaky**

6. _____ **clumsy**

7. _____ **ecstatic**

8. _____ **accusatory**

9. _____ **foolish**

10. _____ **melancholy**

11. _____ **obnoxious**

12. _____ **spendthrift**

13. _____ **crabby**

A. "Where are we? I thought this was . . . no, I guess not," stuttered Stan.

B. "I don't think I can walk another step," sighed Sanders, falling into a nearby recliner.

C. Stomping his feet, Sean shrieked, "You can't make me finish my work!"

D. "Shh! Get your head down, Sarah. Don't let Mrs. Lions see us," whispered Wanda.

E. "Oops! I'm sorry. I thought you were my brother," moaned Martha as she wiped ketchup off the waiter's white shirt.

F. "Uhhh. Four . . . no, seven . . .Uhh. Is this true or false, Miss Jacobs?" inquired Isaac.

G. "No, just go ahead to the movie without me. I think I'll just stay home and cry myself to sleep," croaked Craig.

H. "Oh, how wonderful! My very own Darby Delight Dollhouse!" squealed Skeeter.

I. "Hey, I just stepped on your feet. Oops! I did it again!" giggled Garth.

J. "Aww come on, Ron! You must have eaten that blueberry pie. You've got crumbs on your chin and a stain on your shirt," observed Oscar.

K. "Leave me alone! Just get out of my face!" shouted Sheri.

L. "Hey there's another penny! That makes 42 cents I've saved this week," muttered Mindy.

M. "What a dump! Hey string bean! Get over here and take my order," demanded Damion.

GO

© Frank Schaffer Publications

DIRECTIONS: Evaluate the story descriptions below. Choose the answer that would be the most contrived, or least realistic, plot for the story that is described.

Clue   Remember that a contrived plot is one in which the conflict is wrapped up too easily or with a very unlikely coincidence.

14. Jack and Andrew are hopelessly lost in the desert. They have run out of food and have only a little water. After two nights of walking, they _____ .

   (A) happen upon a group of nomads who care for them

   (B) find an oasis with water, dried food, and an abandoned satellite phone

   (C) find a stray camel who carries them to civilization

   (D) are awakened by the sound of the search party's helicopter

15. Jayda leaves home determined to make it as an actress in New York. She auditions for many plays but is not offered any parts. Finally she is down to her last $10. She then _____ .

   (F) finds a job as a waitress and enrolls in acting lessons

   (G) meets a man who is directing a play and needs an actress for the starring role

   (H) decides to move to Hollywood instead

   (J) calls her parents to bring her home and abandons her hopes of stardom

16. The crop has failed for the second year in a row. The bank is about to take the farm. Then, one day _____ .

   (A) Jacob is hoeing in the field and strikes oil. The family is rich beyond imagination

   (B) Aunt Matilda's will, which has been missing for a year, is found in a book. She has left the family enough money to pay off their debts

   (C) the entire community comes together to donate enough money for the family to keep the farm

   (D) Jacob begs the bank manger to give him one last chance to pay his debts, and the manager agrees to wait one more year

STOP

© Frank Schaffer Publications

Name _____ Date _____

Selecting Favorite Authors and Genres

DIRECTIONS: What are your three favorite genres of reading (science fiction, historical romance, poetry, sports stories, etc.)? For each genre, name your favorite work, give the author's name, and write a brief summary of the book.

Favorite genre: _____

    Favorite work in this genre: _____

    Author's name: _____

    Brief summary: _____

    _____

    _____

    _____

    _____

Second-favorite genre: _____

    Favorite work in this genre: _____

    Author's name: _____

    Brief summary: _____

    _____

    _____

    _____

    _____

Third-favorite genre: _____

    Favorite work in this genre: _____

    Author's name: _____

    Brief summary: _____

    _____

    _____

    _____

    _____

DIRECTIONS: Which author have you read the most? Name all of the works you have read by this author and briefly tell why you like this author's writing so much.

_____

_____

_____

_____

_____

_____

_____

_____

_____

_____

_____

_____

_____

_____

_____

_____

_____

_____

_____

_____

STOP

Reading

Connecting Texts to Historical Context

DIRECTIONS: Read the poems and answer the questions that follow.

The Death of the Ball Turret Gunner

From my mother's sleep I fell into the State,
And I hunched in its belly till my wet fur froze.
Six miles from earth, loosed from its dreams of life,
I woke to black flak and the nightmare fighters.
When I died they washed me out of the turret with
    a hose.

1. **About which of the following events do you think this poem was written?**

    (A) the assassination of Abraham Lincoln

    (B) the Civil War

    (C) World War II

    (D) the Wright Brothers' flight at Kitty Hawk

2. **Identify some images from the poem that tell you that a ball turret is part of an airplane.**

    _____

    _____

    _____

    _____

    _____

    _____

    _____

from Concord Hymn

By the rude bridge that arched the flood,
    Their flag to April's breeze unfurled,
Here once the embattled farmers stood
    And fired the shot heard round the world.

The foe long since in silence slept;
    Alike the conqueror silent sleeps;
And Time the ruined bridge has swept
    Down the dark stream which seaward creeps.

3. **This poem commemorates the Battles of Lexington and Concord, which occurred on April 19, 1775. These battles were part of**

    _____ .

    (F) the American Civil War

    (G) the War of 1812

    (H) World War I

    (J) the American Revolutionary War

4. **To whom is the poet referring in the line "The foe long since in silence slept"?**

    (A) the Union soldiers who fought in the Civil War

    (B) the British who fought in the Revolutionary War

    (C) the Native Americans who lived in the United States at the time of the Revolution

    (D) the settlers who first came to America

© Frank Schaffer Publications

Name _____ Date _____

Reading

2B.4

Read and
Understand
Literature

Making Connections

DIRECTIONS: Read the passage and then answer the questions on the next page.

Mummies Have No Secrets

Mummies cannot hide their age. They cannot hide what they ate for their last meals or whether their families were wealthy or poor. Mummies cannot hide much of anything from anthropologists.

Wrappings and artifacts reveal much about the social status of the person while alive. For example, a mummy found in the Taklimakan Desert sported a bronze earring and leather boots. The decorations on these items showed that his people were skilled artisans.

A mummy's body reveals even more clues than its wrappings. The contents of a mummy's digestive tract can be examined chemically and microscopically, giving anthropologists clues about the person's diet. When anthropologist studied the Iceman, a mummy found in Italy, they examined the contents of his intestines. They wanted to see what he ate in the hours before his death. Organs and bones reveal details about the way the person died, too. Even if no flesh remains, bones and teeth might reveal the age of the person at death, as well as some details about diet, height, occupation, ethnicity, and social status. A male mummy's worn front teeth might indicate that he used his teeth to hold a tool, freeing his hands for other work. In addition, since bone absorbs minerals during a person's life, a chemical study of the bones turns up information about the diet of the deceased person. If DNA can be extracted from a mummy, scientists can even determine the blood type of the deceased person.

Even death and 5,000 years cannot hide a mummy's secrets. These secrets are contributing to what we know about ancient life.

1. **What is the main idea of the passage?**

   (A) Modern science can help us learn about ancient human life.

   (B) Ancient people ate the same things we did.

   (C) People used to dress very differently than we do.

   (D) Anthropologists studied the Iceman.

2. **A mummy found in which desert wore a bronze earring?**

   (F) Tulsa Desert

   (G) Taklimakan Desert

   (H) Egyptian Desert

   (J) Sahara Desert

3. **Scientific testing may allow us to know all but which one of the following?**

   (A) We may know if the person had a disease.

   (B) We may know exactly how old the person was when they died.

   (C) We may know if the person enjoyed listening to music.

   (D) We may know if the person took a medicine.

4. **Which sentence below is not a fact based on the passage?**

   (F) A mummy's digestive tract can be examined.

   (G) Wrappings and artifacts reveal much about the mummy's life.

   (H) Scientists believe that mummies can be cloned with DNA.

   (J) The Iceman was found in Italy.

5. **If the following sentences were placed in order, which one would be number two?**

   (A) A chemical reaction helps determine what the mummy ate.

   (B) The digestive tract is examined with chemicals.

   (C) A mummy is found in the Taklimakan Desert.

   (D) The mummy is taken to a research facility.

6. **Which of the following would not give us a clue as to the mummy's social status?**

   (F) food

   (G) clothes

   (H) jewelry

   (J) height

7. **If your family lived in a culture that practiced mummification, what artifacts would scientists find about you and your family?**

   _____

   _____

   _____

   _____

   _____

   _____

   _____

   _____

   _____

   _____

© Frank Schaffer Publications

Reading

| 2B.5 |

Recurring Themes in Print and Media

DIRECTIONS: Select an important issue of the day. Find and read or watch three different stories about it. (Possible sources include newspapers, magazines, TV reports, or Internet articles.) Then answer the following questions.

1. What is the subject of the stories?

_____

_____

2. What are the main facts regarding the issue?

_____

_____

_____

_____

3. What are the points of agreement among the stories? Points of disagreement?

_____

_____

_____

_____

_____

_____

_____

_____

_____

4. Do any of the stories contain more or less detail about certain aspects of the story? Explain.

_____

_____

_____

_____

_____

_____

_____

_____

5. What is the tone of each story (neutral, objective, optimistic, skeptical, etc.)? Support your evaluation with specific evidence.

_____

_____

_____

_____

_____

_____

_____

_____

_____

Reading

2B.6

Comparing Works From Different Times and Places

DIRECTIONS: Visit the library or go online to find information about the works listed in the table below. For each work, identify the genre and the culture where it originated. Then pick one of the works, find a copy online or at the library, and read it. Compare it to something else you've read recently.

	Genre	Culture
Beowulf		
Anansie tales		
The Twenty-Two Goblins		
The Two Frogs		
The Nose		
A Modest Proposal		
The Animals Sick of the Plague		
Ode on a Grecian Urn		

Title of historical work:

_____

_____

_____

Title of recently read work:

_____

_____

_____

What are some basic similarities and differences in the themes, plot, and language between the two works?

_____

_____

_____

_____

_____

_____

_____

_____

© Frank Schaffer Publications

Name _____ Date _____

Read and
Understand
Literature

Making Inferences and Drawing Conclusions

DIRECTIONS: Read the story and then answer the questions on the next page.

Trouble Is My Middle Name

I'll admit, the list is long. I broke Mom's favorite blue vase playing baseball in the house. True, it was a home run, but that didn't count much with Mom. I broke the back window. I really didn't think I could break a window by shoving my hip against a door. Probably bad glass. I ruined the living room carpeting with a red spot the size of a basketball right in the middle of the entryway. I know the rules: no drinking in the living room. But I wasn't really drinking in there. I didn't even get a taste before I spilled the glass full of red juice.

I guess "Trouble" is my middle name. At least that's what Mom says. So, you won't be surprised when I tell you I'm in trouble once again. This time, it really wasn't my fault.

I invited the guys over. Just a little game of baseball in the backyard. Joe was the one who wanted to put home plate where we would be hitting directly at the Banters' house. I made them turn it so we were hitting into their garden. This time, I was thinking. No more broken windows!

Well, you can guess what happened. Joe hit a home-run ball that went deep. I chased it out of the yard right into the Banters' garden. I caught it, too. I also destroyed three tomato plants and fell into the corn. It could have happened to anyone. It didn't have to be me, but remember my middle name. Trouble just haunts me. Mrs. Banter wasn't so nice about the plants. She said I had to buy her some fresh tomatoes in August to replace

her harvest. She didn't say much about the corn, but she has plenty more corn plants.

I apologized as best I could and helped her repair some of the plants. We used sticks to help prop them up. It was pretty much the end of our game, though.

Mom was glad I apologized. She said I could do extra chores to earn money to buy tomatoes for Mrs. Banter. She said I should slow down and think before I do things.

These days, I play baseball only at the park. I'm working hard to find a different middle name.

© Frank Schaffer Publications

95

1. **About how old do you think the narrator is? How can you tell?**

   _____

   _____

   _____

   _____

   _____

   _____

2. **How did the narrator feel when he asked the guys to hit toward Mrs. Banter's garden rather than her house?**

   (A) clever

   (B) malicious

   (C) embarrassed

   (D) confused

3. **How do you know? Cite a specific example from the text.**

   _____

   _____

   _____

   _____

   _____

4. **How long ago do you think this incident occurred?**

   (F) within a few days

   (G) several months ago

   (H) a couple of years ago

   (J) many years ago; the narrator is now an adult and is recounting a story from his childhood

5. **How do you know? Cite a specific example from the text.**

   _____

   _____

   _____

   _____

   _____

   _____

6. **Do you think the narrator of the story will be able to change? Why or why not?**

   _____

   _____

   _____

   _____

   _____

STOP

© Frank Schaffer Publications

Reading

2B.8

Impact of Word Choice on Content

DIRECTIONS: In the story, several different words are used in place of *ran* and *screamed*. See if you can find them and then list them below.

Score!

It was one of the closest games of the season. The teams were so evenly matched that neither team had been able to score. Time was running out. No score would mean overtime, but one good kick could mean winning the game.

Justin dashed down the soccer field toward the goal. "I'm open!" he shouted. "Pass the ball." He scanned the field around him, searching for a player from his team. "Brian, over here!"

Brian kicked the ball toward Justin, but before Justin could reach it, one of the opponents darted in and booted the ball away.

"Don't worry. We'll get it next time," yelled the coach as Brian sprinted back to regain possession of the ball.

This time, Brian dribbled out the wing, beating opponent after opponent. He centered the ball, and Justin bolted up just in time to kick it toward the goal. It was caught by the goalie. The goalie threw the ball back into play.

"Nice try! You almost had it!" shouted the coach as the team rushed back down the field.

The opponents now had possession of the ball. They flew past the first defender, took a shot at the goal, and missed.

"Make this one count!" bellowed the goalie as he kicked the ball out to his team.

Brian was determined to score. The game was nearly over, but there was still no score on the board. If either team could score a point before time was up, they would win the game. He raced down the field. He could hear the fans in the background. "Go! Score!" they roared.

In a last effort, the whole team charged down to help him out. They passed the ball around the opponents and worked closer and closer to the goal. Justin passed the ball to Brian, who took aim at the goal and gave it a mighty kick. The shot was good! The team had won!

"Congratulations! You guys were great! What a game! What a team!" cheered the fans.

Justin beamed with pride as he and the other players headed off the field.

1. ran:

_____

_____

_____

2. screamed:

_____

_____

_____

DIRECTIONS: In the space below, tell how the variety of word choices you identified above enhance the story.

3. _____

_____

_____

_____

_____

_____

_____

STOP

Supporting Interpretations With Textual Evidence

DIRECTIONS: Read the story and then answer the questions on the next page.

What If?

We were settled in our sleeping bags after a really bad day.

We went fishing in the morning with Toby—after breakfast, of course—just off the dock. But that was enough. The monster of the lake pulled me into the water three times, although Toby says I'm just faking it. I'm not faking! There's a monster fish in this lake. I'm never going to swim here again—ever!

This afternoon, I had archery class. I got two bull's-eyes that didn't count just because they were on another kid's target! Then came camping skills class. We learned how to make a stew over a campfire. How was I supposed to know the can would be so hot? I dropped the can and put out the fire. What a bunch of crybabies those other kids are!

Well, like I said, we had just settled down in bed when I happened to look out the window. It's hard to believe any animal in its right mind would want to live in such a dark, scary place. So, I was checking things out to see if everything was okay. I caught a glimmer of something big and shadowy. It was so big its shadow blotted out all the moonlight.

When I saw that shadow, I got a little bit scared. Well, I was scared enough to poke my head down into my sleeping bag and clamp the top of the bag closed with my fist. And when Toby left us, because he wanted to be with the other counselors, I started worrying.

What would I do if a huge owl swooped down?

What if the owl smashed through the window?

And grabbed me?

And flew away with me in its claws?

Who would tell my parents?

I almost wanted to cry. I used to do that a lot. But I didn't this time. It's not a good idea to cry around other guys. Somebody might laugh.

I was getting a little hot inside my sleeping bag. I opened my fist. I popped my head out. No one else was making a sound, other than the deep-sleep breathing sounds of all the other kids in the cabin. I looked out the window.

And there it was.

© Frank Schaffer Publications

DIRECTIONS: Name and briefly describe the five major events in the plot of "What If?"

1. _____

   _____

   _____

   _____

2. _____

   _____

   _____

   _____

   _____

3. _____

   _____

   _____

   _____

   _____

4. _____

   _____

   _____

   _____

5. _____

   _____

   _____

   _____

DIRECTIONS: For questions 6–8, support your answers with specific evidence from the text.

6. **Of what is the boy most afraid?**

   _____

   _____

7. **How does the author bring the element of suspense into this plot?**

   _____

   _____

   _____

   _____

   _____

8. **The conclusion is missing from this story. What do you think the narrator saw? Support your idea with evidence from the story.**

   _____

   _____

   _____

   _____

   _____

   _____

   _____

   _____

   _____

STOP

Reading

2.B

For pages 87–99

Mini-Test 5

DIRECTIONS: Read the following story and then answer the questions.

Daedalus

According to a Greek myth, Daedalus was an inventor who had a son named Icarus. Daedalus designed the labyrinth, a maze of complicated passages that is very difficult to escape. Minos, the king of the island Crete, used the labyrinth to hide a monster called Minotaur, who was half man and half bull.

Daedalus did something to anger Minos, and the king made Daedalus and Icarus prisoners in the labyrinth. One day, Daedalus got an idea as he was watching birds fly. He asked Icarus to gather up all the bird feathers he could find. Then, using the feathers and some wax, Daedalus created two large pairs of wings. Soon he and Icarus were on their way over the walls of the labyrinth.

1. **Which of the following stories do you think is most likely to have some of the same themes as the story about Daedalus and Icarus?**

   (A) "My Sunny Greek Adventure"

   (B) "The Great Jailbreak"

   (C) "The Birdwatcher"

   (D) "A Family Feud"

2. **Which of the following best describes Icarus?**

   (F) a Greek prince

   (G) a supernatural creature

   (H) a rebellious child

   (J) an innocent captive

3. **Which of the following was most likely the source of Daedalus's ideas for inventions?**

   (A) Greek architecture

   (B) the world of nature

   (C) books and drawings

   (D) the suggestions of King Minos

4. **Write your own version of the Daedalus myth based on the information in the passage. Use the style and tone of a fable or folktale.**

   _____

   _____

   _____

   _____

   _____

   _____

   _____

   _____

   _____

   _____

   _____

© Frank Schaffer Publications

How Am I Doing?

Mini-Test 1

Page 19

Number Correct

[   ]

7–8 answers correct	**Great Job!** Move on to the section test on page 103.
5–6 answers correct	**You're almost there!** But you still need a little practice. Review the practice pages 8–18 before moving on to the section test on page 103.
0–4 answers correct	**Oops!** Time to review what you have learned and try again. Review the practice section on pages 8–18. Then retake the test on page 19. Now move on to the section test on page 103.

Mini-Test 2

Page 46

Number Correct

[   ]

6 answers correct	**Awesome!** Move on to the section test on page 103.
4–5 answers correct	**You're almost there!** But you still need a little practice. Review the practice pages 21–45 before moving on to the section test on page 103.
0–3 answers correct	**Oops!** Time to review what you have learned and try again. Review the practice section on pages 21–45. Then retake the test on page 46. Now move on to the section test on page 103.

Mini-Test 3

Page 67

Number Correct

[   ]

6–7 answers correct	**Great Job!** Move on to the section test on page 103.
4–5 answers correct	**You're almost there!** But you still need a little practice. Review the practice pages 49–66 before moving on to the section test on page 103.
0–3 answers correct	**Oops!** Time to review what you have learned and try again. Review the practice section on pages 49–66. Then retake the test on page 67. Now move on to the section test on page 103.

How Am I Doing?

Mini-Test 4 Page 84 **Number Correct**	**7–8** answers correct	**Awesome!** Move on to the section test on page 103.
	4–6 answers correct	**You're almost there!** But you still need a little practice. Review the practice pages 70–83 before moving on to the section test on page 103.
	0–3 answers correct	**Oops!** Time to review what you have learned and try again. Review the practice section on pages 70–83. Then retake the test on page 84. Now move on to the section test on page 103.
Mini-Test 5 Page 100 **Number Correct**	**4** answers correct	**Great Job!** Move on to the section test on page 103.
	3 answers correct	**You're almost there!** But you still need a little practice. Review the practice pages 87–99 before moving on to the section test on page 103.
	0–2 answers correct	**Oops!** Time to review what you have learned and try again. Review the practice section on pages 87–99. Then retake the test on page 100. Now move on to the section test on page 103.

© Frank Schaffer Publications

Final Reading Test
for pages 8–99

DIRECTIONS: Choose the best answer.

1. Which of the following is a simile?

- (A) The bread was not as soft as it should have been.
- (B) The bread was left out and became stale.
- (C) The bread was as hard as a rock.
- (D) The bread was delicious with strawberry jam.

2. Which of the following is a metaphor?

- (F) His harsh words were difficult for Dana to take.
- (G) His words were hammers, pounding at Dana.
- (H) Dana was upset by his harsh words.
- (J) His harsh words made Dana's head pound.

DIRECTIONS: Choose the word that correctly completes both sentences.

3. What's all that _____?
He hit the ball with his _____ .

- (A) noise
- (B) bat
- (C) commotion
- (D) racket

4. The stars _____ at night.
You _____ to be ill.

- (F) seem
- (G) pretend
- (H) appear
- (J) shine

DIRECTIONS: Read the passage, then choose the word that best fits each blank.

Laughter is good medicine. Scientists believe that laughter _____ **(5)** the heart and lungs. Laughter burns calories and may help _____ **(6)** blood pressure. It also _____ **(7)** stress and tension. If you are _____ **(8)** about an upcoming test, laughter can help you relax.

5.
- (A) heals
- (B) stresses
- (C) weakens
- (D) strengthens

6.
- (F) raise
- (G) lower
- (H) eliminate
- (J) elongate

7.
- (A) relieves
- (B) increases
- (C) revives
- (D) releases

8.
- (F) excited
- (G) enthusiastic
- (H) nervous
- (J) knowledgeable

GO

© Frank Schaffer Publications

DIRECTIONS: Read the passage, then answer the questions.

The practice of wearing rings is a very ancient one. Throughout history, people in many lands have decorated their bodies by wearing rings on their fingers, ears, lips, necks, noses, ankles, and wrists. In some cultures, a married woman wore a ring on the big toe of her left foot; a man might have put rings on his second and third toes. Today, the practice of wearing rings in some cases includes multiple facial rings, as well as rings in many other areas of the body.

9. What is the paragraph mainly about?

- Ⓐ why some people wore rings on their toes
- Ⓑ what kinds of rings were the most popular
- Ⓒ when the practice of wearing rings began
- Ⓓ how people throughout history have worn rings

10. Which title best summarizes this passage?

- Ⓕ "Rings Worn Today"
- Ⓖ "Rings Throughout the Ages"
- Ⓗ "Rings in Unusual Places"
- Ⓙ "Rings Are Fun"

DIRECTIONS: Choose the word that means the same or about the same as the underlined word.

11. surprising outcome

- Ⓐ relationship
- Ⓑ appointment
- Ⓒ result
- Ⓓ announcement

12. hideous mask

- Ⓕ lovely
- Ⓖ funny
- Ⓗ monstrous
- Ⓙ false

13. audible sigh

- Ⓐ heard
- Ⓑ silent
- Ⓒ austere
- Ⓓ angry

14. desolate landscape

- Ⓕ forested
- Ⓖ barren
- Ⓗ desirable
- Ⓙ unnatural

15. To subside is to _____ .

- Ⓐ continue
- Ⓑ grow louder
- Ⓒ cease
- Ⓓ be intermittent

16. A cunning plan is _____ .

- Ⓕ clever
- Ⓖ unoriginal
- Ⓗ mistaken
- Ⓙ detailed

DIRECTIONS: Read the passage, then answer the questions.

Maternal Fish Father

In the warm and temperate waters of the world live two unusual fish: the sea horse and its relative, the pipefish.

The sea horse, so-called because its head resembles a horse, is a small fish about two to eight inches long. It swims by moving the dorsal fin on its back. It is the only fish with a prehensile tail that it uses, like a monkey, to coil around and cling to seaweed.

The pipefish is named for its long snout, which looks like a thin pipe. When its body is straight, the pipefish resembles a slender snake. Its body forms an *S* shape and is propelled by its rear fins.

GO ⇨

© Frank Schaffer Publications

Name _____   Date _____

But it is not appearance that makes the sea horse and pipefish unique. It is their paternal roles. With both fish, the female's responsibility ends when she lays and deposits her eggs. From that point on, the male takes over and, in a manner of speaking, gives birth to the babies.

Both the male sea horse and pipefish have pouch-like organs on their undersides in which the female deposits her eggs. Here the young fish stay and are nourished for either a few days or for several weeks, depending on the species. When the baby sea horses are ready to be born, the father sea horse attaches itself to a plant and actually goes through the pangs of childbirth. As the sea horse bends back and forth, the wall of its brood pouch contracts. With each spasm, a baby fish is introduced into the world of the sea. The birth of the baby pipefish is less dramatic. The father's pouch simply opens, and the offspring swim off on their own.

17. What is the main idea of this passage?

- (A) The pipefish and the sea horse fathers are unusual because of the way their offspring are born.
- (B) Sea horses resemble horses but have tales like monkeys.
- (C) Female pipefish and sea horses are lazy.
- (D) Sea horses make good pets.

18. Which statement does not describe a sea horse?

- (F) The sea horse's head resembles a horse.
- (G) The sea horse's body is propelled by a rear fin.
- (H) The sea horse uses its snout to cling to seaweed.
- (J) The sea horse has a prehensile tail.

DIRECTIONS: Read the story and answer questions 19–24.

In the Frigid Wilderness

That grueling night lingered on and on. I was not a stranger to the below-zero temperatures, the frightening howls of the wolves, nor the wind's wail through the majestic fir trees. However, at 15 years old, my lack of experience had decreased my chance of survival on that harsh and bitter night.

I had set out that day to check and reset my animal traps. I waited an extra day for the snowstorm to subside for two reasons: I did not want to meet any ravenous wild animals foraging for food, and I thought my trapping business would be more profitable if I allowed the game more time to hunt. I prepared a sack lunch and put on my hunting belt complete with a hatchet and bullets for my gun. My dog Kenai, part malamute and part wolf, waited impatiently at the door while I packed. This was Kenai's first all-day outing.

Kenai enjoyed the smell of beaver, mouse, and chipmunk. We collected potential pelts that would be sold to the fur traders, ate lunch, and tramped in the woods for hours. At dusk, I knew we should venture home. I whistled for Kenai. Bang! Bang! Suddenly Kenai's cry erupted through the frigid air and fear pierced my heart.

Minutes seemed like hours as I ran to Kenai. My best friend lay in a pool of his own blood, breathing a low, throaty growl. Now I was the one who was frightened! He depended on me to save his life.

Trying to stay calm and rational, I made a plan. With my knowledge of first aid, I fashioned a makeshift tourniquet out of my hunting belt to stop the bleeding. Next, I would attempt to take Kenai home. But how?

I decided to make a sled from tree limbs and the inner lining of my parka. I frantically slashed away at the limbs, slipped them inside the lining, zipped it up, and stuffed it with boughs. Cautiously I laid Kenai in the middle, hoping my idea would be successful. Dragging the heavy dog in the frigid night took a toll on my body. The familiar sounds of the forest kept me moving until I dropped from sheer exhaustion. I decided to rest for just a minute. I woke up from a deep sleep startled to hear human voices. Dad and a rescue team had followed my trap lines and found us barely breathing, but conscious!

Neither Kenai nor I will ever forget that night. But because of it, the wolf-like dog and I share a bond of friendship that few people, or dogs, ever experience.

© Frank Schaffer Publications

19. **What could be another title for this story?**

    Ⓐ *A Harrowing Hunting Trip*

    Ⓑ *Fun in the Woods*

    Ⓒ *Dad Saves All!*

    Ⓓ *Kenai, the Wonder Dog!*

20. **Which of the following was not packed for the trip?**

    Ⓕ hatchet

    Ⓖ sack lunch

    Ⓗ first-aid kit

    Ⓙ bullets

21. **The narrator of the story probably did not have previous knowledge of what?**

    Ⓐ first-aid

    Ⓑ using a gun

    Ⓒ setting traps

    Ⓓ saving a dog's life

22. **Which of the following is an opinion based on the information in the story?**

    Ⓕ The narrator spends time outdoors.

    Ⓖ The narrator knows how to use a gun.

    Ⓗ The narrator probably gets good grades in school.

    Ⓙ The narrator cares for his dog.

23. **The author of this story builds suspense by _____ .**

    Ⓐ saying the character has a gun

    Ⓑ saying that the character's dad rescued him

    Ⓒ describing the struggles of the character and his dog

    Ⓓ letting the reader know the dog was frightened

24. **Which of the following events would be last if placed in order?**

    Ⓕ Remove the lining from the coat.

    Ⓖ Drag the injured animal to safety.

    Ⓗ Stuff the lining with boughs and limbs from a tree.

    Ⓙ Place the injured animal on the lining.

STOP

© Frank Schaffer Publications

Name _____   Date _____

Final Reading Test
Answer Sheet

1 (A) (B) (C) (D)
2 (F) (G) (H) (J)
3 (A) (B) (C) (D)
4 (F) (G) (H) (J)
5 (A) (B) (C) (D)
6 (F) (G) (H) (J)
7 (A) (B) (C) (D)
8 (F) (G) (H) (J)
9 (A) (B) (C) (D)
10 (F) (G) (H) (J)

11 (A) (B) (C) (D)
12 (F) (G) (H) (J)
13 (A) (B) (C) (D)
14 (F) (G) (H) (J)
15 (A) (B) (C) (D)
16 (F) (G) (H) (J)
17 (A) (B) (C) (D)
18 (F) (G) (H) (J)
19 (A) (B) (C) (D)
20 (F) (G) (H) (J)

21 (A) (B) (C) (D)
22 (F) (G) (H) (J)
23 (A) (B) (C) (D)
24 (F) (G) (H) (J)

Illinois Mathematics
Content Standards

The mathematics section of the state test measures knowledge in five different areas.

Goal 3: Demonstrate and apply a knowledge and sense of numbers, including numeration and operations, patterns, ratios, and proportions.

Goal 4: Estimate, make, and use measurement of objects, quantities, and relationships and determine acceptable levels of accuracy.

Goal 5: Use algebraic and analytical methods to identify and describe patterns and relationships in data, solve problems, and predict results.

Goal 6: Use geometric methods to analyze, categorize, and draw conclusions about points, lines, planes, and space.

Goal 7: Collect, organize, and analyze data using statistical methods; predict results; and interpret certainty using concepts of probability.

Illinois Mathematics
Table of Contents

© Frank Schaffer Publications

Mathematics Standards

Number Sense

Goal 3: Demonstrate and apply a knowledge and sense of numbers, including numeration and operations, patterns, ratios, and proportions.

Learning Standard 3A—Students who meet the standard can demonstrate knowledge and use of numbers and their many representations in a broad range of theoretical and practical settings. *(Representations)*

1. Represent place values from units through billions using powers of ten. *(See page 111.)*
2. Represent, order, compare, and graph integers. *(See page 112.)*

What it means:
- An **integer** is any whole number or its opposite. For example, 2, −2, 6, or 100 are integers.

3. Identify fractional pieces that have the same value but different shapes. *(See page 113.)*
4. Compare and order fractions and decimals efficiently and find their approximate position on a number line. *(See page 114.)*
5. Represent repeated factors using exponents. *(See page 115.)*

Learning Standard 3B—Students who meet the standard can investigate, represent, and solve problems using number facts, operations and their properties, algorithms, and relationships. *(Operations and properties)*

1. Write prime factorizations of numbers. *(See page 116.)*

What it means:
- **Prime factorization** is showing any number as the product of its primes. For example, $16 = 2 \times 2 \times 2 \times 2$ or 2^4 or $36 = 2 \times 2 \times 3 \times 3$ or $2^2 \times 3^2$.

2. Determine the least common multiple and the greatest common factor of a set of numbers. *(See page 117.)*
3. Demonstrate the meaning of multiplication of fractions (e.g., $\frac{1}{2} \times 3$ is $\frac{1}{2}$ of a group of three objects). *(See page 118.)*
4. Simplify simple arithmetic expressions with rational numbers using the field properties and the order of operations. *(See page 119.)*
5. Recognize and use the inverse relationships of addition and subtraction and multiplication and division to simplify computations and solve problems. *(See page 120.)*
6. Solve multiplication number sentences and word problems with whole numbers and familiar fractions. *(See page 121.)*

Mathematics Standards

Learning Standard 3C—Students who meet the standard can compute and estimate using mental mathematics, paper-and-pencil methods, calculators, and computers. *(Choice of method)*

1. Select and use appropriate operations, methods, and tools to compute or estimate using whole numbers with natural number exponents. *(See page 122.)*
2. Analyze algorithms for computing with whole numbers, familiar fractions, and decimals and develop fluency in their use. *(See page 123.)*

What it means:
- An **algorithm** is a generalized procedure or methods for computing or solving a problem.

Learning Standard 3D—Students who meet the standard can solve problems using comparison of quantities, ratios, proportions, and percents.

1. Solve number sentences and word problems using percents. *(See page 124.)*
2. Demonstrate and explain the meaning of percents, including greater than 100 and less than 1. *(See page 125.)*
3. Create and explain a pattern that shows a constant ratio. *(See page 126.)*
4. Analyze situations to determine whether ratios are appropriate to solve problems. *(See page 127.)*
5. Determine equivalent ratios. *(See page 128.)*

What it means:
- A **ratio** is a comparison of one quantity to another.

© Frank Schaffer Publications

Mathematics

3A.1

Representing Place Values Using Powers of Ten

DIRECTIONS: Choose the best answer.

1. The 7 in 68,745 means _____ .

   (A) 7×10^1

   (B) 7×10^2

   (C) 7×10^3

   (D) 7×10^4

2. 4,000,000 equals _____ .

   (F) 4×10^6

   (G) 4×10^7

   (H) 4×10^8

   (J) 4×10^9

3. 3×10^5 equals _____ .

   (A) 30,000,000

   (B) 3,000,000

   (C) 300,000

   (D) 30,000

4. 7,813 equals _____ .

   (F) $(7 \times 10^2) + (8 \times 10^2) + 10^2 + 3^2$

   (G) $(7 \times 10^4) + (8 \times 10^3) + 10^2 + 3$

   (H) $(7 \times 10^3) + (8 \times 10^2) + 10^1 + 3$

   (J) $(7 \times 10^4) + (8 \times 10^3) + 10^2 + (3 \times 10^1)$

5. One billion is the same as _____ .

   (A) 10^9

   (B) 10^{10}

   (C) 10^{11}

   (D) 10^{12}

6. The 5 in 54,112 means _____ .

   (F) 1×10^5

   (G) 5×10^4

   (H) 10×5^5

   (J) 5×10^3

7. The 4 in 241 means _____ .

   (A) 4×10^1

   (B) 4×10^2

   (C) 4×10^3

   (D) 4×10^4

8. 7×10^4 equals _____ .

   (F) 700

   (G) 7,000

   (H) 70,000

   (J) 700,000

STOP

© Frank Schaffer Publications

Mathematics

3A.2

Using Integers

DIRECTIONS: Choose the best answer.

1. **Which group of numbers is ordered from greatest to least?**

   (A) 7,834   1,979   7,878   3,876

   (B) 1,234   3,456   5,689   7,893

   (C) 3,456   4,576   4,579   5,423

   (D) 8,778   6,545   2,324   1,645

2. **What number is 2,000 less than 765,422?**

   (F) 565,422

   (G) 765,222

   (H) 763,422

   (J) 745,422

3. **How many even numbers are there between 4 and 24?**

   (A) 6

   (B) 8

   (C) 12

   (D) 9

4. **What number is expressed by (8 × 10,000) + (5 × 1,000) + (3 × 100) + (8 × 1)?**

   (F) 805,308

   (G) 85,308

   (H) 850,308

   (J) 805,380

5. **Which of these numbers is between 5,945,089 and 5,956,108?**

   (A) 5,995,098

   (B) 5,943,787

   (C) 5,947,109

   (D) 5,549,090

6. **How many odd numbers are between 9 and 31?**

   (F) 7

   (G) 9

   (H) 10

   (J) 11

7. **What number is expressed by (6 × 100,000) + (5 × 1,000) + (2 × 10) + (9 × 1)?**

   (A) 6,529

   (B) 65,290

   (C) 605,029

   (D) 650,209

8. **Which of these numbers is between 356,800 and 358,109?**

   (F) 356,690

   (G) 357,240

   (H) 356,790

   (J) 358,200

9. **In the space below, draw a number line and place the following integers in correct order on the line: −3, 9, 0, 4, 12.**

STOP

© Frank Schaffer Publications

Mathematics

3A.3

Equivalent Fractional Pieces of Different Shapes

Number Sense

DIRECTIONS: Choose the best answer.

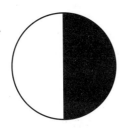

1. Which of the following shows the same fractional value as the figure above?

Ⓐ   Ⓑ

Ⓒ   Ⓓ

2. Which of the following shows the same fractional value as the figure above?

Ⓕ   Ⓖ

Ⓗ   Ⓙ

3. Which of the following shows the same fractional value as the figure above?

Ⓐ   Ⓑ

Ⓒ   Ⓓ

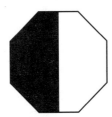

4. Which of the following shows the same fractional value as the figure above?

Ⓕ   Ⓖ

Ⓗ   Ⓙ

STOP

© Frank Schaffer Publications

Name _____   Date _____

Comparing Fractions and Decimals

Number Sense

DIRECTIONS: Use the number line for questions 1–3.

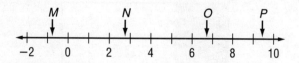

1. **On the number line, which arrow points most closely to 2.8?**

    (A) M

    (B) N

    (C) O

    (D) P

2. **On the number line, which arrow points most closely to $6\frac{3}{4}$?**

    (F) M

    (G) N

    (H) O

    (J) P

3. **On the number line, which arrow points most closely to −0.8?**

    (A) M

    (B) N

    (C) O

    (D) P

4. **Which of these values is between 0.07 and 0.5 in value?**

    (F) 0.18

    (G) 0.81

    (H) 0.007

    (J) 0.018

5. **Which group of decimals is ordered from greatest to least?**

    (A) 3.021, 4.123, 0.788, 1.234

    (B) 0.567, 0.870, 0.912, 1.087

    (C) 2.067, 1.989, 1.320, 0.879

    (D) 0.003, 1.076, 0.873, 0.002

6. **How many of the fractions listed are greater than $\frac{3}{5}$?**

    $$\frac{2}{5}, \frac{3}{4}, \frac{6}{7}, \frac{1}{2}, \frac{20}{25}, \frac{7}{10}$$

    (F) 1

    (G) 3

    (H) 4

    (J) 2

7. **Which of these is between 0.08 and 0.4 in value?**

    (A) 0.19

    (B) 0.91

    (C) 0.009

    (D) 0.019

8. **Which group of decimals is ordered from least to greatest?**

    (F) 4.081, 1.804, 10.48, 1.408

    (G) 1.048, 1.408, 1.804, 4.081

    (H) 0.481, 1.408, 4.801, 0.841

    (J) 0.841, 0.481, 8.401, 8.014

STOP

© Frank Schaffer Publications

Mathematics

3A.5

Using Exponents

DIRECTIONS: Choose the best answer.

1. **Which of these is another way to write 6 × 6 × 6 × 6?**
   - (A) 6×4
   - (B) 64
   - (C) 6^4
   - (D) $6 + 4$

2. **Which of these is another way to write 80?**
   - (F) $2^4 \times 5$
   - (G) 2^4
   - (H) $2^3 \times 20$
   - (J) $2 \times 2 \times 2 \times 5$

3. **What is 77 written as a product of prime numbers?**
   - (A) $7^2 \times 11$
   - (B) 7×11
   - (C) $7 \times 2 \times 11$
   - (D) $7 + 11$

4. **Which of these is another way to write 5 × 5 × 5 × 5 × 5?**
   - (F) 5×5
   - (G) 5^3
   - (H) 5^4
   - (J) 5^5

5. **What is 125 written as a product of prime numbers?**
   - (A) 5×5
   - (B) 5^3
   - (C) 5^4
   - (D) 5^5

6. **The speed of light is 300,000,000 m/s. What is this number in scientific notation?**
   - (F) 3×10^9
   - (G) 3×10^8
   - (H) 3×10^7
   - (J) 3×10^6

7. **The mass of a dust particle is 0.000000000753 kg. What is this number in scientific notation?**
   - (A) 7.53×10^{-10}
   - (B) 0.753×10^{-9}
   - (C) 753×10^{-12}
   - (D) 75.3×10^{-11}

8. **Which of the following is 1.23×10^{11} in standard form?**
   - (F) $123,000,000,011$
   - (G) $123,000$
   - (H) $123,000,000$
   - (J) $123,000,000,000$

9. **75 =**
   - (A) 2×25
   - (B) 3×5^2
   - (C) 3×5^3
   - (D) 15×4

STOP

© Frank Schaffer Publications

3B.1   # Prime Factorizations

DIRECTIONS: Find the prime factorization of each composite number. Write the prime factors in numerical order on the leaves of the factor tree. Check your answers by completing the factor tree.

1. Prime Factorization = _____

2. Prime Factorization = _____

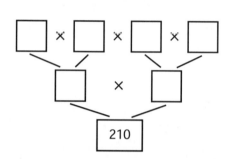

3. Prime Factorization = _____

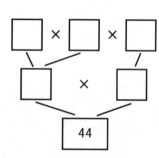

4. Prime Factorization = _____

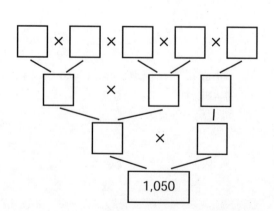

© Frank Schaffer Publications

Mathematics

3B.2

Common
Multiples and Factors

DIRECTIONS: Choose the best answer.

1. **What is the greatest common factor of 42 and 54?**

   Ⓐ 6
   Ⓑ 7
   Ⓒ 4
   Ⓓ 9

2. **What is the greatest common factor of 16 and 64?**

   Ⓕ 4
   Ⓖ 8
   Ⓗ 16
   Ⓙ 2

3. **What is the greatest common factor of 27 and 45?**

   Ⓐ 3
   Ⓑ 7
   Ⓒ 9
   Ⓓ 5

4. **What is the least common multiple of 3, 4, and 6?**

   Ⓕ 6
   Ⓖ 12
   Ⓗ 18
   Ⓙ 24

5. **What is the least common multiple of 5 and 3?**

   Ⓐ 3
   Ⓑ 5
   Ⓒ 15
   Ⓓ 30

6. **What is the least common multiple of 3, 6, and 8?**

   Ⓕ 6
   Ⓖ 12
   Ⓗ 18
   Ⓙ 24

7. **What is the least common multiple of 4, 5, and 10?**

   Ⓐ 20
   Ⓑ 15
   Ⓒ 10
   Ⓓ 5

8. **What is the least common multiple of 4, 6, and 9?**

   Ⓕ 12
   Ⓖ 24
   Ⓗ 36
   Ⓙ 48

STOP

© Frank Schaffer Publications

Mathematics

3B.3

Meaning of Multiplication of Fractions

Number Sense

DIRECTIONS: Choose the best answer.

1. $\frac{1}{2} \times 3$ is the same as _____ .
   - (A) one quarter of a group of three
   - (B) one quarter of a group of nine
   - (C) one half of a group of three
   - (D) none of the above

2. $\frac{1}{2} \times 6$ is the same as _____ .
   - (F) one quarter of a group of twelve
   - (G) one half of a group of six
   - (H) both F and G
   - (J) neither F nor G

3. **Half of the shaded area in the square above is the same as _____ .**
   - (A) $\frac{1}{2} \times 1$
   - (B) $\frac{1}{4} \times 1$
   - (C) $\frac{1}{2} \times \frac{1}{2}$
   - (D) $\frac{1}{2} \times \frac{1}{4}$

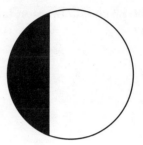

4. **Half of the shaded area in the circle above is the same as _____ .**
   - (F) $\frac{1}{2} \times \frac{1}{3}$
   - (G) $\frac{1}{3} \times 1$
   - (H) $\frac{1}{3} \times \frac{1}{3}$
   - (J) $\frac{1}{2} \times \frac{1}{6}$

5. $\frac{1}{5} \times 5$ is the same as _____ .
   - (A) one half of a group of five
   - (B) one fifth of a group of five
   - (C) two fifths of a group of 25
   - (D) none of the above

6. $\frac{3}{4} \times 2$ is the same as _____ .
   - (F) one quarter of a group of two
   - (G) one half of a group of two
   - (H) three quarters of a group of two
   - (J) none of the above

STOP

© Frank Schaffer Publications

Mathematics

3B.4

Simplifying
Arithmetic Expressions

Number Sense

DIRECTIONS: Choose the best answer.

1. **A simpler way to write (3 × 5) × 6 would be** _____ .

   (A) 8 × 6

   (B) 15 × 6

   (C) 15 + 6

   (D) 8 + 6

2. **A simpler way to write 50 ÷ (4 × 5 − 36 ÷ 2) + −9 would be** _____ .

   (F) 25 + −9

   (G) 50 + −9

   (H) 6.25 + −9

   (J) 42 + 9

3. **A simpler way to write 15 − 8 × 2 + 11 − 5 × 2 would be** _____ .

   (A) 91 − 10

   (B) 7 × 12

   (C) 15 − 16 + 11 − 10

   (D) 14 + 12

4. **A simpler way to write 5(3 + 6) × 2(3 + 2) would be** _____ .

   (F) 45 × 10

   (G) 45 + 10

   (H) 21 × 8

   (J) 21 + 8

5. **A simpler way to write (6 ÷ 2) × 3 would be** _____ .

   (A) 3 ÷ 3

   (B) 3 × 3

   (C) 6 ÷ 6

   (D) 6 ÷ 5

6. **A simpler way to write 2 × (2 ÷ 2) would be** _____ .

   (F) 23

   (G) 4 ÷ 2

   (H) 2 × 1

   (J) none of the above

7. **A simpler way to write (4 × 5) − 5 would be** _____ .

   (A) 4 × −5

   (B) 4 × 0

   (C) 4 × 1

   (D) none of the above

STOP

© Frank Schaffer Publications

Mathematics

3B.5

Using Inverse Relationships

DIRECTIONS: Choose the best answer.

> **Examples:**
>
> An *inverse relationship* is when a pair of operations will undo each other.
>
> Addition and subtraction have an inverse relationship. For example, $2 + 3 = 5$ can also be reversed as $5 - 3 = 2$.
>
> Multiplication and division have an inverse relationship. For example: $2 \times 5 = 10$ can be reversed as $10 \div 5 = 2$.

 Clue Do not work the problems. Use the inverse relationships of addition/subtraction and multiplication/division to solve the problems.

1. If $28{,}153 - 17{,}745 = 10{,}408$ then
   $10{,}408 + 17{,}745 = $ _____ .
   - (A) 7,337
   - (B) 27,153
   - (C) 28,153
   - (D) 38,561

2. If $872 - 593 = 279$ then $279 + 593 = $
   _____ .
   - (F) 872
   - (G) 314
   - (H) 593
   - (J) 558

3. If $x - 355 = y$ then $y + 355 = $ _____ .
   - (A) z
   - (B) y
   - (C) x
   - (D) none of the above

4. If $362 \times 16 = 5{,}792$ then
   $5{,}792 \div 16 = $ _____ .
   - (F) 462
   - (G) 362
   - (H) 1,362
   - (J) 92,192

5. If $a \times b = c$ then $c \div b = $ _____ .
   - (A) a
   - (B) b
   - (C) c
   - (D) x

6. If $x \div y = z$ then $z \times y = $ _____ .
   - (F) x^2
   - (G) y^2
   - (H) z^2
   - (J) none of the above

STOP

© Frank Schaffer Publications

Mathematics

| 3B.6 |

Multiplying Whole Numbers and Fractions

Number Sense

DIRECTIONS: Choose the best answer.

1. Brigida earns $5 an hour. How much will she earn in 10 hours?

- (A) $15
- (B) $25
- (C) $50
- (D) $55

2. A jet traveled at an average speed of 680 kilometers an hour. At that rate, how many kilometers did the jet go in $7\frac{1}{2}$ hours?

- (F) 5,100
- (G) 5,198
- (H) 6,108
- (J) 3,128

3. Milo's car can be driven an average of $21\frac{1}{2}$ miles on each gallon of gasoline. How many miles can his car be driven on 9 gallons of gasoline?

- (A) $112\frac{1}{2}$
- (B) 201
- (C) $193\frac{1}{2}$
- (D) $21\frac{1}{2}$

4. 756 × 432 = _____

- (F) 236,592
- (G) 326,592
- (H) 336,592
- (J) none of the above

5. $\frac{2}{9} \times \frac{7}{8} =$ _____

- (A) $\frac{7}{36}$
- (B) $\frac{16}{63}$
- (C) $\frac{7}{9}$
- (D) none of the above

6. $\frac{2}{5} \times 4 =$ _____

- (F) $1\frac{3}{5}$
- (G) 10
- (H) $1\frac{4}{5}$
- (J) $4\frac{2}{5}$

7. Chris put 16 ounces of jam into jars. He filled 12 jars and had no jam left over. How many ounces of jam did he use?

- (A) 90
- (B) 180
- (C) 192
- (D) none of the above

STOP

Mathematics

| 3C.1 |

Working With Whole Numbers and Exponents

DIRECTIONS: Complete the following exponential equations.

1. $2^3 =$ 3. $3^3 =$ 5. $2^3 \times 2 + 4^2 =$

2. $5^2 =$ 4. $3^2 \times 2^3 =$ 6. $3^3 - 2^3 \times 3 =$

DIRECTIONS: Write an equivalent exponential expression for each of the following numbers.

7. $64 =$ 10. $125 =$ 13. $216 =$

8. $100 =$ 11. $16 =$ 14. $729 =$

9. $25 =$ 12. $243 =$ 15. $343 =$

DIRECTIONS: Find the decimal value for each of the following exponential expressions.

Multiplying or dividing by multiples of 10 moves the decimal point in a number. Mathematicians and scientists use exponents as shorthand for writing these operations.

8.32×10^4

$8.32 \times 10^4 = 8.32 \times 10,000$

$8.32 \quad = 83,200$

Multiplying means moving the decimal to the right. The 4 in the exponent tells us to move the decimal 4 places.

16. $2.4569 \times 10^3 =$ 18. $6.15892 \times 10^5 =$ 20. $6.8 \times 10^4 =$

17. $5.9 \times 10^2 =$ 19. $2.34 \times 10^1 =$ 21. $5.3498 \times 10^6 =$

STOP

© Frank Schaffer Publications

Mathematics

3C.2 | # Analyzing Algorithms

DIRECTIONS: Use the algorithms described below in each example box to choose the best answers.

Example:

One algorithm for dividing fractions is: (1) find a common denominator, (2) rename the fractions, and (3) divide the numerators. *Example:* To find $\frac{10}{12} \div \frac{2}{4}$, find a common denominator: 12; rename the fractions: $\frac{10}{12}$ and $\frac{6}{12}$; and divide the numerators: 10/6.

---

1. $\frac{9}{10} \div \frac{1}{5} =$

(A) $\frac{4}{2}$ (C) $\frac{8}{5}$

(B) $\frac{9}{2}$ (D) $\frac{2}{9}$

2. $\frac{5}{14} \div \frac{1}{2} =$

(F) $\frac{4}{12}$ (H) $\frac{5}{7}$

(G) $\frac{7}{5}$ (J) $\frac{1}{3}$

Example:

One algorithm for converting mixed numbers to fractions is: (1) multiply the whole number and the denominator, (2) add the numerator to the sum to find the new numerator, and (3) place the new numerator over the original denominator. *Example:* To convert $7\frac{1}{3}$ to a fraction, multiply $7 \times 3 = 21$; add the sum to the numerator: $21 + 1 = 22$; and place the new numerator over the original denominator: $\frac{22}{3}$.

---

3. $8\frac{3}{4} =$

(A) $\frac{24}{3}$ (C) $\frac{32}{4}$

(B) $\frac{24}{4}$ (D) $\frac{35}{4}$

4. $7\frac{5}{6} =$

(F) $\frac{35}{6}$ (H) $\frac{42}{6}$

(G) $\frac{35}{5}$ (J) $\frac{47}{6}$

Example:

One algorithm for multiplying two numbers is: (1) break down one of the numbers into a simpler equation, (2) multiply the first number by the new second number, and (3) multiply the result by the new third number. *Example:* To multiply 25×36, break down one of the numbers into a simpler equation: $25 \times 4 \times 9$; multiply the first number by the new second number: $25 \times 4 = 100$; and multiply that result by the new third number: $100 \times 9 = 900$.

---

5. $12 \times 15 =$

(A) 160 (C) 200

(B) 180 (D) 220

6. **20×25 is the same as** _____ .

(F) $20 \times 5 \times 5$

(G) $20 \times 20 \times 5$

(H) $10 \times 10 \times 25$

(J) $20 \times 4 \times 5$

STOP

© Frank Schaffer Publications

Mathematics   **Number Sense**

3D.1   # Percentages

DIRECTIONS: Choose the best answer.

Example:

The enrollment at King School has increased 20% from last year. The enrollment last year was 650. By how many students has the enrollment increased?

(A) 120

(B) 130

(C) 150

(D) 90

Answer: (B)

1. **Pizzazz Pizza Parlor gave the sixth grade class a 25% discount on pizzas they purchased for a party. Each pizza originally cost $12.00. How much did the sixth graders pay per pizza?**

   (A) $3.00

   (B) $9.00

   (C) $8.00

   (D) $6.00

2. **Twenty-five percent of the workers are on third shift. There are 132 workers in all. How many of them are on third shift?**

   (F) 25

   (G) 12

   (H) 33

   (J) 3

3. **The enrollment at Franklin School has increased 20% from last year. The enrollment last year was 750. By how many students has the enrollment increased?**

   (A) 750

   (B) 900

   (C) 600

   (D) 150

4. **Forty percent of the class finished their assignment before lunch. There are 25 students in the class. How many students finished before lunch?**

   (F) 40

   (G) 10

   (H) 25

   (J) 12

5. **The tax on a certain item is 10% of the sale price. What would be the amount of tax on an item that sells for $60?**

   (A) $6

   (B) $10

   (C) $60

   (D) $5

6. **It is estimated that a new truck will be worth 75% of its original cost after one year. How much would a 1-year-old truck be worth that originally sold for $5,600?**

   (F) $5,600

   (G) $1,400

   (H) $4,200

   (J) $4,000

STOP

© Frank Schaffer Publications

Name _____ Date _____

3D.2

Meaning of Percents

DIRECTIONS: Shade the items to indicate the given percent of each collection of objects.

1. 60%

2. 75%

3. 40%

DIRECTIONS: Give the percent of the items shaded in each collection.

4. _____

5. _____

6. _____

DIRECTIONS: Estimate the percent of each bar that is shaded.

7. _____

8. _____

9. _____

DIRECTIONS: Explain whether the following statements make sense or not.

10. Stock prices rose 120%.

_____

_____

_____

11. Gasoline prices fell 110%.

_____

_____

_____

STOP

© Frank Schaffer Publications

Constant Ratios

DIRECTIONS: Choose the best answer.

1. Matt owns 2 blue shirts and 6 red shirts. If he buys 1 new blue shirt, how many red shirts will he need to buy to maintain the same ratio of blue shirts to red shirts?

    (A) 1   (C) 3

    (B) 2   (D) 4

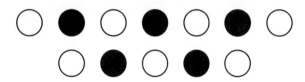

2. The ratio of which of the following patterns is constant with the pattern shown above?

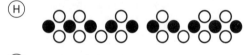

3. 1, 2, 4, 8 is a geometric sequence with a constant ratio of _____ .

    (A) 1   (C) 4

    (B) 2   (D) 8

4. Suppose a geometric sequence has a constant ratio of 3. Which number comes before and after 81?

    (F) before: 27; after: 90

    (G) before: 72; after: 90

    (H) before: 27; after: 243

    (J) before: 78; after: 84

5. 1, 4, 16, 64 is a geometric sequence with a constant ratio of _____ .

    (A) 1   (C) 4

    (B) 2   (D) 8

6. Suppose a geometric sequence has a constant ratio of 5. Which number comes before and after 5?

    (F) before: 1; after: 25

    (G) before: 25; after: 125

    (H) before: 5; after: 25

    (J) before: 1; after: 125

7. The ratio of which of the following patterns is constant with the pattern shown above?

© Frank Schaffer Publications

Name _____   Date _____

Mathematics

3D.4   # Using Ratios to
Solve Problems   **Number Sense**

DIRECTIONS: Analyze the following problems and determine whether they can be solved using ratios. If so, write **Y** in the blank space; if not, write **N**.

 Clue   A **ratio** is a comparison of one quantity to another.

_____ 1. "Now batting for Toledo, Mickey Calavito," the game announcer yells into his microphone. In the last game, Mickey got 1 hit in 4 tries. If he continues to hit at this rate, determine how many hits Mickey can expect to get if he bats 600 times during the season.

_____ 2. The 154 sixth graders at Ellison Middle School sold an average of 38 tickets each to the school's annual raffle, which raises money to buy additional library books. The cost of each raffle ticket was $4. How much money was raised for the library?

_____ 3. Aleesha saved $0.45 out of her allowance for several weeks so that she could buy a bottle of nail polish for $2.70. How many weeks did she need to save $0.45?

_____ 4. Richard sits at a table in the cafeteria with his 7 friends. Usually his friends are all hungry enough to order the full lunch menu, but today, only two of his friends order the full lunch menu. There are 332 students in the cafeteria. If Richard's table is representative of the entire cafeteria, how many students in the cafeteria ordered the full lunch menu?

_____ 5. Forty percent of the class finished their assignment before lunch. There are 25 students in the class. How many students finished before lunch?

_____ 6. Fred is drawing a scale model of a room that is 12 feet by 14 feet. If he makes one side of the room 3 inches, how long should the other side be?

_____ 7. The temperature in Rockville at 7:00 A.M. was 7°C. By 12:00 noon, the temperature increased to 13°C, but it fell by 3°C by 6:00 P.M. How much did the temperature increase between 7:00 A.M. and noon?

_____ 8. Kerri worked out for $1\frac{1}{2}$ hours, Kelly worked out for 2 hours, and Briana worked out for 45 minutes. What was the total workout time for all three women?

STOP

© Frank Schaffer Publications   **127**

Mathematics

3D.5

Equivalent Ratios

DIRECTIONS: Choose the best answer.

1. The ratio of two days to four weeks is equivalent to _____ .

   (A) $\frac{1}{2}$

   (B) $\frac{1}{14}$

   (C) $\frac{1}{7}$

   (D) $\frac{1}{16}$

2. The ratio of the scale drawing of Brittany's bedroom to the actual bedroom is 1 inch to 5 feet. If the width of Brittany's bedroom is 15 feet, what should be the width of the bedroom on the scale drawing?

   (F) 1 inch

   (G) 3 inches

   (H) 5 inches

   (J) 7 inches

3. The ratio of the scale drawing of Brittany's family room to the actual family room is 1 inch to 5 feet. If the length of Brittany's family room is 20 feet, what should be the length of the family room on the scale drawing?

   (A) 2 inches

   (B) 6 inches

   (C) 4 inches

   (D) 8 inches

4. Fred's Building Company is designing a new volleyball court at Heritage High School. The ratio of the scale drawing to the actual court is 1 inch to 5 feet. If the length of the actual court will be 74 feet, what should be the length of the court on the scale drawing?

   (F) 12.6 inches

   (G) 14.8 inches

   (H) 37.5 inches

   (J) 74 inches

5. When it rains 3 inches in an hour at Calistoga Creek, the creek rises $\frac{1}{2}$ inch. If the rise of the water in Calistoga Creek is proportional to the amount of rain the creek receives, how much will the creek rise if it rains 9 inches in an hour?

   (A) 24 inches

   (B) $1\frac{1}{2}$ inches

   (C) $1\frac{1}{3}$ inches

   (D) $\frac{3}{16}$ inches

6. The ratio of boys who play kickball at recess to girls who play kickball at recess is 5 to 8. If there are 20 boys playing kickball, how many girls are playing?

   (F) 32 girls

   (G) 40 girls

   (H) 100 girls

   (J) 160 girls

7. Tara brought 5 cookies, 8 brownies, and 6 cupcakes to a party. Mark brought an equivalent ratio of these goodies to the party. If Mark brought 10 cookies, how many cupcakes did he bring?

   (A) 5

   (B) 6

   (C) 12

   (D) 22

STOP

© Frank Schaffer Publications

Mathematics

3

For pages 111–128

Mini-Test 1

Number Sense

DIRECTIONS: Choose the best answer. Use the number line for questions 1–2.

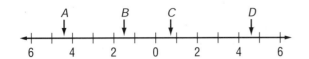

1. **Which letter marks $4\frac{6}{10}$ on this number line?**

   (A) A

   (B) B

   (C) C

   (D) D

2. **Which letter marks -1.5 on this number line?**

   (F) A

   (G) B

   (H) C

   (J) D

3. **During the sale, ladies' coats are selling for 75% of the original price. The original price is $98. What is the sale price of the coats?**

   (A) $24.50

   (B) $73.50

   (C) $98.00

   (D) $75.00

4. **Mrs. James purchased a pair of gloves for 50% off of the regular price of $12.50. How much did she pay for the gloves?**

   (F) $6.25

   (G) $12.50

   (H) $3.25

   (J) $9.25

5. **Find n.** $\dfrac{48}{n} = \dfrac{2}{4}$

   (A) 24

   (B) 96

   (C) 12

   (D) 36

6. **What is the least common multiple of 6 and 9?**

   (F) 3

   (G) 6

   (H) 15

   (J) 18

DIRECTIONS: Use this information for questions 7–8: There are 4 apples, 2 bananas, 5 oranges, and 3 pears in a fruit bowl.

7. **What is the ratio of apples to oranges?**

   (A) 5:4

   (B) $\dfrac{4}{5}$

   (C) 4 to 14

   (D) $\dfrac{9}{5}$

8. **What is not the ratio of bananas to fruit?**

   (F) 2 to 14

   (G) 2:12

   (H) $\dfrac{1}{7}$

   (J) 1:7

9. **$452 \times 73 =$**

   (A) 23,699

   (B) 23,996

   (C) 32,996

   (D) 32,969

10. **$\dfrac{3}{5} \times \dfrac{1}{2} =$**

    (F) $\dfrac{2}{3}$

    (G) $\dfrac{3}{10}$

    (H) 1

    (J) $1\dfrac{1}{5}$

STOP

© Frank Schaffer Publications

Mathematics Standards

Estimate, Make, and Use Measurement

Goal 4: Estimate, make, and use measurement of objects, quantities, and relationships and determine acceptable levels of accuracy.

Learning Standard 4A—Students who meet the standard can measure and compare quantities using appropriate units, instruments, and methods. *(Performance and conversion of measurements)*

1. Investigate the history of the U.S. customary and metric systems of measurement.
2. Measure, with a greater degree of accuracy, any angle using a protractor or angle ruler. *(See page 131.)*

Learning Standard 4B—Students who meet the standard can estimate measurements and determine acceptable levels of accuracy. *(Estimation)*

1. Estimate distance, weight, temperature, and elapsed time using reasonable units and with acceptable levels of accuracy. *(See page 132.)*

Learning Standard 4C—Students who meet the standard can select and use appropriate technology, instruments, and formulas to solve problems, interpret results, and communicate findings. *(Progression from selection of appropriate tools and methods to application of measurements to solve problems)*

1. Select and justify an appropriate formula to find the area of triangles, parallelograms, and trapezoids. *(See page 133.)*
2. Select an appropriate formula or strategy to find the surface area and volume of rectangular and triangular prisms. *(See page 134.)*

What it means:
- **Surface area** is the total area of all faces on a space shape.

3. Develop and use formulas for determining the area of triangles, parallelograms, and trapezoids. *(See page 133.)*
4. Develop and use the formula for determining the volume of a rectangular and triangular prism. *(See page 134.)*
5. Calculate the surface area of a cube, rectangular prism, and triangular prism. *(See page 134.)*
6. Develop and use formulas for determining the circumference and arc of circles. *(See page 135.)*

What it means:
- The **circumference** of a circle is the distance around the outside of the circle. An **arc** is a portion of a circle.

© Frank Schaffer Publications

Name _____ Date _____

Mathematics

4A.2

Measuring Angles

Estimate, Make, and
Use Measurement

DIRECTIONS: Choose the best answer. Use a protractor or angle ruler to measure the angles.

1. **Frank is setting up for a bank shot against LeRoy. The table is set up like the picture below. Frank figures that he needs to bank the ball at an angle between 60° and 80°. Which of the angles below measures between 60° and 80°?**

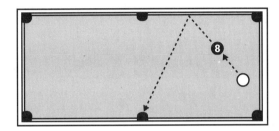

(A)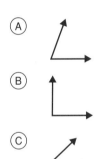

(B)

(C)

(D)

2. **Mrs. Bard, the drama teacher at the middle school, always makes pecan pie during the holiday season. The first and biggest piece goes to the student with the highest grades in her class during the first semester. It is a great honor. Look at the picture below. Vivian Hepburn ate the first piece with well-deserved relish. What is the angle of the first piece of pie?**

(F) 145°
(G) 50°
(H) 35°
(J) 10°

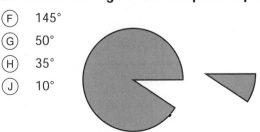

3. **At her little brother's Little League games, most of the fans scream and carry on, caught up in the action of their little players. Cassandra focuses on angles. She loves angles. She plays pool, fishes, and wants to be an architect when she grows up. Cassandra's brother is hitting the ball, but Cassandra is not watching her brother. She is interested only in the angle created by the batted ball. What is the angle created by the pitch coming off the bat as it is hit?**

(A) 20°
(B) 45°
(C) 80°
(D) 140°

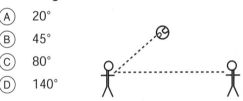

4. **Which of the following angles measures 78°?**

(F)

(G)

(H)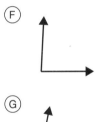

(J)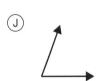

STOP

© Frank Schaffer Publications

131

Mathematics

4B.1

Estimating Measurements

Estimate, Make, and
Use Measurement

DIRECTIONS: Choose the best answer.

1. **Two paper clips weigh about 1 gram. There are 100 paper clips in a box. How many grams would a box of paper clips weigh?**

   (A) 100 g

   (B) 10 g

   (C) 20 g

   (D) 50 g

2. **Anthony's trampoline is about 3 yards across. About how many inches across is his trampoline?**

   (F) 108 inches

   (G) 36 inches

   (H) 54 inches

   (J) 30 inches

3. **On Highway 52, it is about 30 miles from Smallville to Sunnydale, 27 miles from Sunnydale to Riverside, 18 miles from Riverside to Macon, and 6 miles from Macon to Lake Andrew. About how far is it from Sunnydale to Lake Andrew?**

   (A) 80 miles

   (B) 75 miles

   (C) 50 miles

   (D) 25 miles

4. **You go to bed at 10:10 P.M. You are excited because in about 11 hours you are leaving for a vacation. Which clock shows about what time you will be leaving for your vacation?**

   (F)

   (G)

   (H)

   (J)

5. **What temperature will the thermometer show if the temperature rises 12°?**

   (A) −15°

   (B) −9°

   (C) 9°

   (D) 15°

   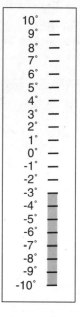

6. **A soccer game started at 11:10 A.M. and lasted $1\frac{1}{2}$ hours. About what time did the game end?**

   (F) 12:30 P.M.

   (G) 1:30 P.M.

   (H) 12:00 A.M.

   (J) 1:00 A.M.

STOP

© Frank Schaffer Publications

Mathematics

4C.1/4C.3

Area of Polygons

DIRECTIONS: Find the area of each polygon below. Include the correct units in your answers.

Clue

Triangle:	Area = $\frac{1}{2}$ bh	b = base
Rectangle:	Area = bh	h = height
Parallelogram:	Area = bh	
Trapezoid:	Area = $\frac{1}{2}$ h(base 1 + base 2)	

Remember, the base and height must be perpendicular.

1.

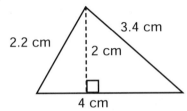

2.2 cm   3.4 cm   2 cm   4 cm

Area: _____

2.

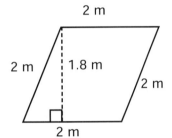

2 m   2 m   1.8 m   2 m   2 m

Area: _____

3.

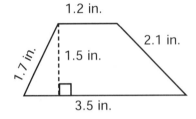

1.2 in.   2.1 in.   1.7 in.   1.5 in.   3.5 in.

Area: _____

4.

12 ft.

4 ft.

Area: _____

5.

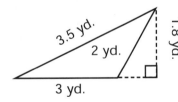

3.5 yd.   2 yd.   1.8 yd.   3 yd.

Area: _____

6.

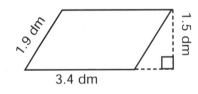

1.9 dm   1.5 dm   3.4 dm

Area: _____

STOP

© Frank Schaffer Publications

Name _____   Date _____

Surface Area and Volume of Cubes and Prisms

Estimate, Make, and
Use Measurement

DIRECTIONS: Choose the best answer.

1. **Which of the following shapes is a triangular prism?**

    Ⓐ

    Ⓑ

    Ⓒ (cylinder)

    Ⓓ (pentagonal prism)

2. **Which of the following shapes is a rectangular prism?**

    Ⓕ

    Ⓖ

    Ⓗ (cube)

    Ⓙ (pentagonal prism)

3. **The formula for the surface area of a rectangular prism, triangular prism, or cube is _____ .**

    Ⓐ $b \times l \times 2$

    Ⓑ $\frac{1}{2} b \times h$

    Ⓒ $\frac{1}{2} b \times l$

    Ⓓ the sum of the areas of the faces

4. **The formula for the volume of a triangular prism is _____ .**

    Ⓕ $l \times w \times h$

    Ⓖ $\frac{1}{2} b \times h$

    Ⓗ $\frac{1}{2} b \times h \times l$

    Ⓙ s^3

5. **The formula for the volume of a rectangular prism is _____ .**

    Ⓐ $l \times w \times h$

    Ⓑ $\frac{1}{2} b \times h$

    Ⓒ $\frac{1}{2} b \times h \times l$

    Ⓓ s^3

6. **Find the volume of a triangular prism with base = 4 cm, height = 5 cm, and length = 8 cm.**

    Ⓕ 160 cm^3

    Ⓖ 80 cm^3

    Ⓗ 40 cm^3

    Ⓙ 10 cm^3

7. **Find the volume of a cube with height = 5 cm, width = 5 cm, and depth = 5 cm.**

    Ⓐ 15 cm^3

    Ⓑ 30 cm^3

    Ⓒ 125 cm^3

    Ⓓ 250 cm^3

8. **What is the volume of a rectangular prism with a length of 8 feet, a height of 6 feet, and a width of 2 feet?**

    Ⓕ 16 cubic feet

    Ⓖ 18 cubic feet

    Ⓗ 96 cubic feet

    Ⓙ 32 cubic feet

9. **Find the surface area of a rectangular prism with length = 8 inches, height = 4 inches, and width = 7 inches.**

    Ⓐ 244 inches^2

    Ⓑ 232 inches^2

    Ⓒ 361 inches^2

    Ⓓ 19 inches^2

STOP

© Frank Schaffer Publications

Name _____ Date _____

Mathematics

4C.6

Circumference and Arc of Circles

DIRECTIONS: Find the circumference and area of each circle below. Include the appropriate units in your answer.

Example:

The **circumference** of a circle is the distance around the outside of the circle. The diameter of a circle is labeled *d*. The radius of a circle is labeled *r*. The diameter is two times the radius (*d=2r*).

The formula for the circumference (*C*) of a circle is C = π*d*. The value of π is 3.14. To figure the circumference of a circle, you would multiply the diameter by 3.14. For example, you have a circle with a circumference of 28 cm. To find the circumference:
    C = π*d* = 3.14 x 28 = 87.92cm

The formula to find the arc length of an angle is *n*/360*C*. The *n* is the angle of an arc and the *C* is the circumference of the circle. The circumference of the circle in the example above was 87.92cm. To find the arc length of a 90° angle within that circle:
    (90 ÷ 360) × 87.92 = 21.98cm

28 cm

d | *r*

d = 2r

1.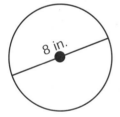
8 in.

2.
100 mm

3.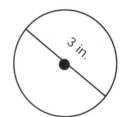
3 in.

4.
20 ft.

5.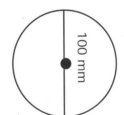
0.8 cm

6.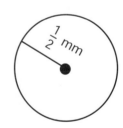
$\frac{1}{2}$ mm

DIRECTIONS: For the circles below, find the arc length for each of the angles. Include the appropriate units in your answer.

7.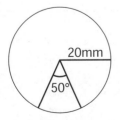
20mm
50°

8.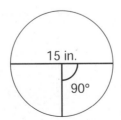
15 in.
90°

9.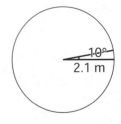
10°
2.1 m

STOP

© Frank Schaffer Publications

Mathematics

For pages 131–135

Mini-Test 2

DIRECTIONS: Choose the best answer.

1. **If you mix 12 ounces of flour and 6 ounces of sugar, how much will it weigh all together?**

   (A) 19 ounces

   (B) 6 ounces

   (C) 72 ounces

   (D) none of the above

2. **A tank of water holds 50 kiloliters. If 1 liter of water weighs 1 kilogram, how many kilograms would the water in the tank weigh?**

   (F) 50,000

   (G) 5,000

   (H) 500

   (J) 50

3. **When Terri Ann read the instructions that came with her skyrocket kit, she learned that the rocket would travel farthest if launched at an angle between 45° and 75°. Which of the angles shown below would not be a good launch angle?**

   (A)

   (B)

   (C)

   (D)

4. **The circumference of a circle with a radius of 12 can be written as _____ .**

   (F) $\pi \times 12^2$

   (G) $\pi \times 2^2 \times 12$

   (H) $\pi \times 2 \times 12$

   (J) $\pi \times 12$

5. **What is the circumference of a circle with a radius of 10?**

   (A) $\pi \times 2 \times 10$

   (B) $\pi \times 10$

   (C) $\pi \times 2^2 \times 10$

   (D) $\pi \times 10^2$

6. **What is the area of a triangle with a base of 5 inches and a height of 10 inches?**

   (F) 15 inches^2

   (G) 25 inches^2

   (H) 50 inches^2

   (J) 20 inches^2

7. **What is the volume of a rectangular prism with a length of 6 feet, a height of 4 feet, and a width of 3 feet?**

   (A) 36 cubic feet

   (B) 288 cubic feet

   (C) 72 cubic feet

   (D) 216 cubic feet

8. **Find the volume of a triangular prism with a base of 12 ft., height of 10 ft., and length of 6 ft.**

   (F) 720 ft.^{3}

   (G) 270 ft.^{3}

   (H) 180 ft.^{3}

   (J) 360 ft.^{3}

STOP

© Frank Schaffer Publications

Mathematics Standards

Use Algebraic and Analytical Methods

Goal 5: Use algebraic and analytical methods to identify and describe patterns and relationships in data, solve problems, and predict results.

Learning Standard 5A—Students who meet the standard can describe numerical relationships using variables and patterns. *(Representations and algebraic manipulations)*

1. Investigate, extend, and describe arithmetic and geometric sequences of numbers whether presented in numeric or pictorial form. *(See page 139.)*
2. Evaluate algebraic expressions for given values. *(See page 140.)*
3. Express properties of numbers and operations using variables (e.g., the commutative property is $m + n = n + m$). *(See page 141.)*

What it means:
- A **variable** is an amount that is not known. It is often represented by a letter.

4. Simplify algebraic expressions involving like terms. *(See page 142.)*

Learning Standard 5B—Students who meet the standard can interpret and describe numerical relationships using tables, graphs, and symbols. *(Connections of representations including the rate of change)*

1. Graph simple inequalities on a number line. *(See page 143.)*

What it means:
- An **inequality** is a sentence with $<$, $>$, $\leq$, or $\geq$ as its verb. Simple inequalities have only one inequality sign.

2. Create a table of values that satisfies a simple linear equation and plot the points on the Cartesian plane. *(See page 144.)*

What it means:
- The **Cartesian plane** is a plane with a rectangular coordinate system that associates each point in the plane with a pair of numbers.

3. Describe, verbally, symbolically, and graphically, a simple relationship presented by a set of ordered pairs of numbers. *(See page 145.)*

Learning Standard 5C—Students who meet the standard can solve problems using systems of numbers and their properties. *(Problem solving)*

1. Identify and explain incorrect uses of the commutative, associative, and distributive properties. *(See page 146.)*

What it means:
- The **commutative property** says you can switch the order of the numbers and still get the same answer.
- The **associative property** says you can change the grouping of the numbers and still get the same answer.
- The **distributive property** is used when there is a combination of multiplication over addition or subtraction.

2. Identify and provide examples of the identity property of addition and multiplication. *(See page 147.)*

What it means:
- The **identity property of addition** states that the sum of any number and zero is the original number ($5 + 0 = 5$).
- The **identity property of multiplication** states that the product of any number and one is that number ($5 \times 1 = 5$).

3. Identify and provide examples of inverse operations. *(See page 147.)*

What it means:
- **Inverse operations** are operations that undo each other.

4. Explain why division by zero is undefined.

Learning Standard 5D—Students who meet the standard can use algebraic concepts and procedures to represent and solve problems.

1. Create, model, and solve algebraic equations using concrete materials. *(See page 148.)*
2. Solve linear equations, including direct variation, with whole number coefficients and solutions using algebraic or graphical representations. *(See page 149.)*

What it means:
- When two variable quantities have a constant (unchanged) ratio, their relationship is called a **direct variation**.

© Frank Schaffer Publications

Mathematics

5A.1

Number Sequences

DIRECTIONS: Choose the best answer.

1. **How are the numbers in Row 1 related to the numbers in Row 2?**

ROW 1	16	24		40	48		64
ROW 2	2	3		5	6		8

(A) Each number is divided by 2.

(B) Each number is multiplied by 4 and then divided by 2.

(C) Each number is divided by 6.

(D) Each number is divided by 8.

2. **What two numbers are missing from Row 1 in question 1?**

(F) 32 and 42

(G) 4 and 7

(H) 4 and 32

(J) 32 and 56

3. **Jalisa observes geese landing at a local pond. 15 land the first day, 20 the second day, 10 the third day, 15 the fourth day, and 5 the fifth day. Jalisa next tried a lake just outside of town. On the third day at this lake, she saw 85 geese and on the fourth day she saw 90 geese. If the pattern at the lake is the same as the pattern at the pond, how many geese did Jalisa see on the first day at the lake?**

Day	Pond	Lake
1	15	
2	20	
3	10	85
4	15	90
5	5	

(A) 15 geese

(B) 80 geese

(C) 90 geese

(D) 95 geese

4. **How many geese did she see the fifth day at the lake?**

(F) 15 geese

(G) 80 geese

(H) 90 geese

(J) 95 geese

5. **What number is missing from the following pattern?**

3, 8, 18, ___, 78, 158

(A) 28

(B) 24

(C) 38

(D) 34

STOP

© Frank Schaffer Publications

Mathematics

5A.2

Algebraic Expressions

DIRECTIONS: Choose the best answer.

 Clue Look for key words, numbers, and figures in each problem, and be sure you perform the correct operation.

1. **A desk normally costs $129. It is on sale for $99. How much would you save if you bought 2 desks on sale?**

   (A) ($129 + $99) × 2 = s

   (B) ($129 − $99) ÷ 2 = s

   (C) ($129 − $99) × 2 = s

   (D) ($129 + $99) ÷ 2 = s

2. **The highway department uses 6 gallons of paint for every 10 blocks of highway stripe. How many gallons will be needed for 250 blocks of highway stripe?**

   (F) (6 × 10) + 250 = g

   (G) 250 − (10 ÷ 6) = g

   (H) 250 × 10 × 6 = g

   (J) (250 ÷ 10) × 6 = g

3. **A hiker started out with 48 ounces of water. She drank 9 ounces of water after hiking 5 miles and 16 more when she reached mile marker 8. How many ounces of water did she have left?**

   (A) 48 − (9 + 16) = w

   (B) 48 + (9 − 16) = w

   (C) (16 − 9) + 48 = w

   (D) 48 + (9 + 16) = w

4. **Evaluate 2a − 3b + 4c, if a = 4, b = 3, and c = 2.**

   (F) 25

   (G) 38

   (H) 7

   (J) 12

5. **Evaluate 5g + 2h, if g = 1 and h = 4.**

   (A) 13

   (B) 28

   (C) 22

   (D) 7

6. **A barrel is 36 inches from top to bottom. The water in the barrel is $12\frac{1}{2}$ inches deep. How much space is there from the surface of the water to the top of the barrel?**

   (F) $s = 36 \div 12\frac{1}{2}$

   (G) $s = 36 \times 12\frac{1}{2}$

   (H) $s = 36 - 12\frac{1}{2}$

   (J) $s = 36 + 12\frac{1}{2}$

For exercise 7 use the following information. The base of Sandy Mountain is 5,400 feet above sea level. The top of the mountain is 10,700 feet above sea level. A trail runs from the base of the mountain to the top. The trail is 8 miles long, and it takes about 5 hours to hike from the base of the mountain to the top.

7. **Which of the following equations could be used to determine the vertical distance from the base of the mountain to the top?**

   (A) t − b = 5,300

   (B) t + b = 16,100

   (C) t × b = 57,780,000

   (D) t ÷ b = 1.98

STOP

© Frank Schaffer Publications

Mathematics

5A.3

Using Variables

DIRECTIONS: Choose the best answer.

 Clue   A **variable** is an amount that is not known. It is often expressed by a letter.

1. a(b + c) = _____

(A) a × b + a × c

(B) a × b + b × c

(C) a × b × c

(D) none of the above

2. a + b = _____

(F) b + c

(G) c + d

(H) b + a

(J) b − a

3. (a + b) + c = _____

(A) c − (a + b)

(B) a + (b + c)

(C) a × (b + c)

(D) a + (b × c)

4. (a × b) × c = _____

(F) a × (b + c)

(G) a + (b × c)

(H) a × (b × c)

(J) (a × c) − b

5. If x > y and y > z, then _____ .

(A) x < z

(B) x > z

(C) z > x

(D) x = z

6. If y > 98 and y < 123, which of the following is a possible value of y?

(F) 124

(G) 108

(H) 97

(J) 221

7. Which statement is true if b is a whole number?

(A) If b − 8 = 16, then 8 + b = 16

(B) If 8 × b = 16, then 16 ÷ b = 8

(C) If 8 ÷ b = 16, then 16 × 8 = b

(D) If 8 + b = 16, then 16 + 8 = b

STOP

© Frank Schaffer Publications

Name _____ Date _____

Mathematics

5A.4

Simplifying
Algebraic Expressions

**Use Algebraic and
Analytical Methods**

DIRECTIONS: Simplify the following expressions. Choose the best answer.

 Clue   To help determine if your answer is correct, substitute a number for each of the variables in the problem and solution, and calculate the answers.

1. $2x + 3y - 2 + 3x + 6y + 7$
   - (A) $x + 3y + 5$
   - (B) $x + 3y - 5$
   - (C) $5x + 9y - 5$
   - (D) $5x + 9y + 5$

2. $3b + (4b - 6b + 2) + b$
   - (F) $b + 2$
   - (G) $6b - 2$
   - (H) $5b - 2$
   - (J) $4b + 2$

3. $36a^5b^4 \div 9a^3b$
   - (A) $36a^2b^3$
   - (B) $4a^2b^3$
   - (C) $4a^8b^5$
   - (D) $8a^5b^4$

4. $4a - 4b + 3 + 2a + 5b + 2$
   - (F) $6a + 9b + 1$
   - (G) $a + b + 5$
   - (H) $6a + b + 5$
   - (J) $6a + 9b + 5$

5. $4x - (2x - 6x + 5)$
   - (A) $8x - 5$
   - (B) $4x - 5$
   - (C) $4x + 5$
   - (D) $8x + 5$

6. $5x + 4x - 5 + 3x$
   - (F) $12x - 5$
   - (G) $10x + 5$
   - (H) $10x - 5$
   - (J) $12x + 5$

7. $25a^4 \div 5a^3$
   - (A) $5a^4$
   - (B) $25a$
   - (C) $5a$
   - (D) $25a^4$

8. $3x + 2y + 5 + x - y - 4$
   - (F) $4x + y - 1$
   - (G) $4x + 3y - 2$
   - (H) $4x + 3y + 1$
   - (J) $4x + y + 1$

STOP

142

© Frank Schaffer Publications

Mathematics

5B.1

Graphing
Simple Inequalities

DIRECTIONS: For each question, shade the correct points on the number line to solve the inequality.

> **Clue** To solve an inequality is to find all values of the variable that make the inequality true.

1. **On this number line, shade all the points on the line where $x + 2 < 7$.**

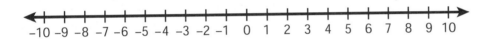

2. **On this number line, shade all the points on the line where $x > 5$.**

3. **On this number line, shade all the points on the line where $x \geq 5$.**

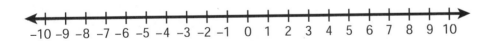

4. **On this number line, shade all the points on the line where $x + 2 < -3$.**

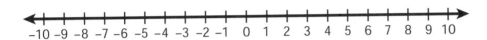

5. **On this number line, shade all the points on the line where $x + 6 \geq -4$.**

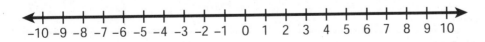

STOP

© Frank Schaffer Publications

Name _____ Date _____

5B.2 Creating a Table of Values and Plotting Points for Linear Equations

Use Algebraic and Analytical Methods

DIRECTIONS: Solve each problem.

Clue The **Cartesian plane** is a plane with a coordinate system that associates each point on the plane with a pair of numbers. The first number in the pair identifies the point on the x-axis and the second number identifies the point on the y-axis.

1. **For the linear equation y = 3X + 2, find the corresponding y values when X = −3, −2, −1, 0, 1, 2, and 3. Show the results as a table of values.**

x							
y							

2. **Plot the points on the Cartesian plane for the equation given in question 1.**

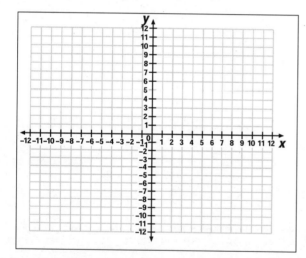

4. **Plot the points on the Cartesian plane for the equation given in question 3.**

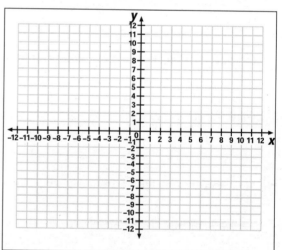

3. **For the linear equation y = 2X, find the corresponding y values when X = −3, −2, −1, 0, 1, 2, and 3. Show the results as a table of values.**

x							
y							

STOP

© Frank Schaffer Publications

Name _____ Date _____

Mathematics
5B.3

Ordered Pairs

Use Algebraic and
Analytical Methods

DIRECTIONS: Choose the best answer.

1. **What are the coordinates of Point *A*?**

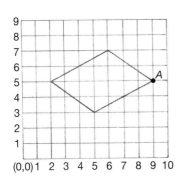

- (A) (2, 5)
- (B) (5, 3)
- (C) (9, 5)
- (D) (6, 7)

DIRECTIONS: Use the following graph for questions 2–5.

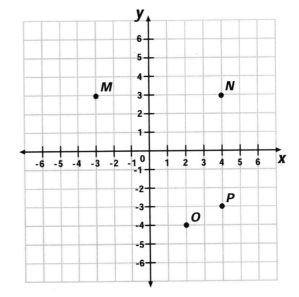

2. **What point is at (−3, 3)?**
- (F) *M*
- (G) *N*
- (H) *O*
- (J) *P*

3. **What point is at (4, 3)?**
- (A) *M*
- (B) *N*
- (C) *O*
- (D) *P*

4. **What are the coordinates of point *P*?**
- (F) (4, 3)
- (G) (4, −3)
- (H) (−3, 4)
- (J) (−4, 3)

5. **Which point represents the answer to the linear equation y = x − 6?**
- (A) *M*
- (B) *N*
- (C) *O*
- (D) *P*

STOP

Mathematics

5C.1

Incorrect Uses of Properties

DIRECTIONS: Answer each question.

Clue The **commutative property** says you can switch the order of the numbers and still get the same answer. The **associative property** says you can change the grouping of the numbers and still get the same answer. The **distributive property** is used when there is a combination of multiplication over addition or subtraction.

1. Barbara thinks that, according to the associative property, $4 + 5 \times 3$ is equal to $3 + 4 \times 5$. Explain why Barbara is wrong.

_____

_____

_____

_____

_____

_____

_____

_____

2. Isaiah believes that, according to the communicative property, $20 - 17$ is the same as $17 - 20$. Explain why Isaiah is wrong.

_____

_____

_____

_____

_____

_____

_____

DIRECTIONS: Choose the best answer.

3. According to the distributive property, which of the following is the same as $5(x + 3)$?

   (A) $5x + 3$

   (B) $5x + 5 \times 3$

   (C) $5 + 3x$

   (D) $5x - 3$

4. According to the distributive property, which of the following is the same as $2(7x + 4) - 5$?

   (F) $2(7) + (x + 4) - 5$

   (G) $2(7x) + 2(-1)$

   (H) $2(7x) + 2(4) - 5$

   (J) $2(7x) + 2(4) - (2 \times 5)$

5. The communicative property applies to which types of operations?

   (A) addition

   (B) multiplication

   (C) division

   (D) both A and B but not C

6. Identify the property that makes the number sentence $46 + 78 = 78 + 46$ true.

   (F) distributive

   (G) communicative

   (H) both F and G

   (J) neither F nor G

STOP

© Frank Schaffer Publications

Name _____   Date _____

Mathematics
5C.2/5C.3

Identity and Inverse Properties

DIRECTIONS: Indicate if the equation illustrates the identity property of addition or multiplication by writing a **Y** in the appropriate space. If it does not, writing an **N** in the appropriate space.

 Clue   The **identity property of addition** states that the sum of any number and zero is the original number. The **identity property of multiplication** states that the product of any number and one is that number. And **inverse operations** are operations that undo each other.

_____ 1. 5 + 0 = 5

_____ 2. 5 + 7 = 7 + 5

_____ 3. 18 × 1 = 18

_____ 4. 0 + a = a

_____ 5. 5(4 + 5) = (5 × 4) + (5 × 5)

_____ 6. 32 = 9

_____ 7. 3 + (5 + 7) = (3 + 5) + 7

_____ 8. a × 1 = a

_____ 9. a + (−a) = 0

DIRECTIONS: Write the inverse of each of the following.

14. + 7   _____

15. − 15   _____

16. + 3   _____

17. × 7   _____

18. − 34   _____

19. ÷ 9   _____

20. × 2   _____

DIRECTIONS: Complete the table below by identifying the inverse operation of the operation shown in the first column.

	Operation	Inverse Operation
10.	+	
11.	−	
12.	×	
13.	÷	

STOP

© Frank Schaffer Publications

Mathematics

Using Models to Solve Equations

Use Algebraic and Analytical Methods

DIRECTIONS: Choose a variable for the unknown amount. Then write a number sentence to represent the problem. Finally, draw a model that illustrates the equation and solution, and fill in the solution on the appropriate line.

1. **Kyle made a dozen cookies. His little sister ate 5 of them. How many cookies are left?**

   Variable: Let ____ = _____

   Number sentence: _____

   Model:

   Solution: ____ (variable) = ____

2. **Austin earned 8 dollars more than Reese earned. Reese earned 2 dollars. How much did Austin earn?**

   Variable: Let ____ = _____

   Number sentence: _____

   Model:

   Solution: ____ (variable) = ____

3. **Logan brought three times as many CDs to a party as Jordan brought. Jordan brought three CDs. How many CDs did Logan bring?**

   Variable: Let ____ = _____

   Number sentence: _____

   Model:

   Solution: ____ (variable) = ____

© Frank Schaffer Publications

5D.2

Solving
Linear Equations

DIRECTIONS: Choose the best answer.

1. **What is the value of z in the equation $12 \times z = 144$?**

    (A) 8

    (B) 12

    (C) 122

    (D) 11

2. **What is the value of x if $54 \div x = 9$?**

    (F) 7

    (G) 6

    (H) 63

    (J) 45

3. **What is the value of r if $17 \times r = 68$?**

    (A) 51

    (B) 4

    (C) 85

    (D) 6

4. **What is the value of a in the equation $(7 \times a) - 9 = 54$?**

    (F) 8

    (G) 7

    (H) 5

    (J) 9

5. **If $z + 8 = 31$, then $z =$**

    (A) 39

    (B) 23

    (C) 22

    (D) 4

6. **Your uncle bought 375 feet of wire fencing. He put up 325 feet today and saved the rest for tomorrow. Which equation shows how many feet of fencing he has left?**

    (F) $375 + f = 325$

    (G) $375 - 325 = f$

    (H) $f = 375 + 325$

    (J) $375 - f = 325$

7. **If 27 students each brought in 6 cookies, which equation shows how many cookies they brought in all?**

    (A) $27 + 6 = c$

    (B) $27 \times 6 = c$

    (C) $27 - 6 = c$

    (D) $27 \div 6 = c$

8. **Which equation shows the total attendance at the Science Fair if 67 girls and 59 boys attended?**

    (F) $67 - 59 = a$

    (G) $67 + 59 = a$

    (H) $67 \div 59 = a$

    (J) $67 \times 59 = a$

9. **Sergio spent $3.80 on heavy-duty string for his project. He bought 20 feet of string. Which equation could you use to find out the price per foot of the string?**

    (A) $\$3.80 + 20 = s$

    (B) $\$3.80 - 20 = s$

    (C) $\$3.80 \times 20 = s$

    (D) $\$3.80 \div 20 = s$

STOP

© Frank Schaffer Publications

Mathematics

5

For pages 139–149

DIRECTIONS: Choose the best answer.

1. Consider the table of values shown. The relationship of *x* to *y* is represented by which equation?

x	0	1	2	3	4
y	2	5	8	11	14

- Ⓐ $y = 4x$
- Ⓑ $y = x + 2$
- Ⓒ $y = 3x + 2$
- Ⓓ $y = 4x - 1$

2. The line is the graph for—

- Ⓕ $x = y$
- Ⓖ $x = y + 4$
- Ⓗ $x = 8y$
- Ⓙ $x = y + 2$

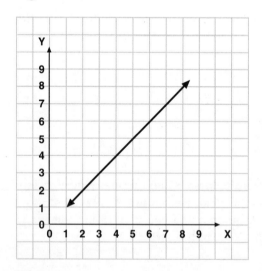

3. Evaluate $3x - y$ if $x = 4$ and $y = 1$.

- Ⓐ 11
- Ⓑ 12
- Ⓒ 6
- Ⓓ 9

4. Mrs. Wacker looked at the chart below to determine how many ounces of chocolate mint sauce she needed to prepare for the vanilla bean pie her guests will enjoy at her dinner party.

Servings	1	2	3	4	5
Ounces of Sauce Needed	2	4	6	8	10

Mrs. Wacker has invited 6 guests who will each get 1 serving of her famous dessert. She also plans to make 12 extra ounces of sauce to give to one of the guests to take home. Which expression can be used to determine how many ounces of chocolate mint sauce Mrs. Wacker needs to make?

- Ⓕ $12 + (2 \times 6)$
- Ⓖ $(12 + 2) \times 6$
- Ⓗ $(2 \times 12) + (8 \times 6)$
- Ⓙ $6 \times (2 + 8) + 12$

5. What number is missing from the pattern below?

$\frac{1}{5}$, 0.3, $\frac{4}{10}$, 0.5, _____, 0.7

- Ⓐ $\frac{5}{10}$
- Ⓑ 6.0
- Ⓒ $\frac{6}{10}$
- Ⓓ 0.06

6. What should replace the ▇ in the number sentence below?

$3 \times 6 = (3 \times 4) + (3 \times ▇)$

- Ⓕ 2
- Ⓖ 3
- Ⓗ 1
- Ⓙ 6

STOP

© Frank Schaffer Publications

Mathematics Standards

Use Geometric Methods

Goal 6: Use geometric methods to analyze, categorize, and draw conclusions about points, lines, planes, and space.

Learning Standard 6A—Students who meet the standard can demonstrate and apply geometric concepts involving points, lines, planes, and space. *(Properties of single figures, coordinate geometry, and constructions)*

1. Plot and read ordered pairs of numbers in all four quadrants. *(See page 153.)*
2. Describe sizes, positions, and orientations of shapes under transformations, including dilations. *(See page 154.)*

What it means:
- A **dilation** is a transformation that produces an image that is the same shape as the original but is a different size.

3. Perform simple constructions (e.g., equal segments, angle and segment bisectors, or perpendicular lines, inscribing a hexagon in a circle) with a compass and straightedge or a mira. *(See page 155.)*
4. Determine and describe the relationship between pi, the diameter, the radius, and the circumference of a circle. *(See page 156.)*
5. Determine unknown angle measures using angle relationships and properties of a triangle or a quadrilateral. *(See page 157.)*

Learning Standard 6B—Students who meet the standard can identify, describe, classify, and compare relationships using points, lines, planes, and solids. *(Connections between and among multiple geometric figures)*

1. Determine the relationships between the number of vertices or sides in a polygon, the number of diagonals, and the sum of its angles. *(See page 158.)*

What it means:
- A **diagonal** is a line segment that connects non-adjacent vertices in a polygon.

2. Solve problems that involve vertical, complementary, and supplementary angles. *(See page 159.)*

What it means:
Students should know definitions of types of angles:
- **Vertical** angles are congruent angles on opposite sides of the same vertex.
- **Complementary** angles are two angles whose sum is 90°.
- **Supplementary** angles are two angles whose sum is 180°.

© Frank Schaffer Publications

3. Analyze quadrilaterals for defining characteristics. *(See page 160.)*

What it means:
- A **quadrilateral** is any four-sided shape.

4. Create a three-dimensional object from any two-dimensional representation of the object, including multiple views, nets, or technological representations.

Learning Standard 6C—Students who meet the standard can construct convincing arguments and proofs to solve problems. *(Justifications of conjectures and conclusions)*

1. Make, test, and justify conjectures about various quadrilateral and triangle relationships, including the triangle inequality. *(See page 161.)*

What it means:
- The **triangle inequality** states that the length of any side of a triangle is less than or equal to the sum of the lengths of the other two sides, with equality occurring only when the triangle degenerates to a line.

2. Justify the relationship between vertical angles. *(See page 162.)*
3. Justify that the sum of the angles of a triangle is 180 degrees. *(See page 162.)*

© Frank Schaffer Publications

Name _____ Date _____

Plotting and Reading Ordered Pairs

Use Geometric Methods

DIRECTIONS: Use the following graph for questions 1–3.

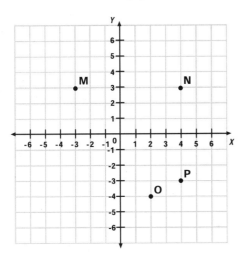

DIRECTIONS: Use the grid for questions 4–5.

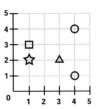

4. **Which of these are the coordinates of the square?**

   F (1, 2)   H (1, 3)

   G (3, 2)   J (4, 4)

5. **Which of these are the coordinates of the star?**

   A (1, 2)   C (1, 3)

   B (3, 2)   D (4, 4)

1. **Which point is at (4, −3)?**

   A   M

   B   N

   C   O

   D   P

6. **Use the grid below to plot the points indicated. Label correctly.**

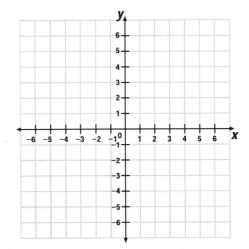

2. **Which point is at (−3, 3)?**

   F   M

   G   N

   H   O

   J   P

3. **What are the coordinates of O?**

   A   (−3, 3)

   B   (2, −4)

   C   (−2, 4)

   D   (−2, −4)

F   (5, 2)   H   (3, −1)

G   (−2, 5)   J   (−6, −4)

© Frank Schaffer Publications

Transformations

DIRECTIONS: Compare the following images to their transformation images. What type of transformation was performed? Be as specific as possible.

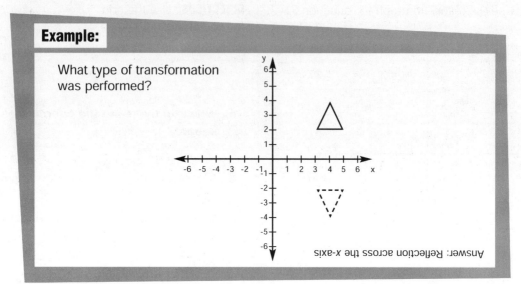

Example:

What type of transformation was performed?

Answer: Reflection across the x-axis

1.

_____

2.

_____

3.

_____

4.

_____

5.

_____

6.

_____

STOP

© Frank Schaffer Publications

Mathematics

6A.3

Performing
Simple Constructions

**Use Geometric
Methods**

DIRECTIONS: Perform the constructions as indicated using a compass, straightedge, or mira, as needed.

Clue
The radius of a circle can be struck exactly six times around the circle. Find the radius with your compass, then set the point of the compass on the circle. Make a mark across the circle, move the point of your compass to that mark, and make another mark across the circle. Connecting each successive intersection with lines will produce a six-sided figure or hexagon.

1. Inscribe a hexagon in the circle below.

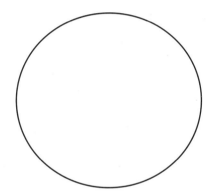

3. Construct the perpendicular bisector of segment AB below.

A •———————————————————• *B*

2. Construct an angle bisector of the angle below.

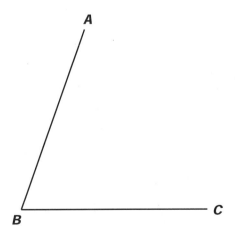

STOP

© Frank Schaffer Publications

Mathematics

6A.4 # Relationship Between Pi, Diameter, Radius, and Circumference

Use Geometric Methods

DIRECTIONS: Select the best answer. Use the provided circle for reference as needed.

d = Diameter: 28 cm
r = Radius: 14 cm
Pi: 3.14
Circumference: 87.92 cm

d
r

1. **The circumference of a circle is ___ times its diameter.**
   - (A) 2
   - (B) 3.14
   - (C) 14
   - (D) none of the above

2. **The radius of a circle is ___ times its diameter.**
   - (F) 14
   - (G) 3.14
   - (H) 2
   - (J) 0.5

3. **Pi represents the _____ .**
   - (A) circumference of a circle divided by its radius
   - (B) diameter of a circle multiplied by its radius
   - (C) circumference of a circle divided by its diameter
   - (D) radius of a circle divided by its diameter

4. **Diameter = _____**
   - (F) 2 × radius
   - (G) 3.14 × radius
   - (H) circumference ÷ radius
   - (J) 2 × pi

5. **Diameter = _____**
   - (A) pi x radius
   - (B) circumference ÷ pi
   - (C) circumference × pi
   - (D) none of the above

STOP

© Frank Schaffer Publications

Name _____ Date _____

Finding the Measurement of Unknown Angles

DIRECTIONS: Look at each triangle. Write the type of triangle (*right*, *acute* or *obtuse*) on the line. Then, write the measurement of the missing angle. The first one is done for you.

 Clue The angle measures in a triangle always add up to 180°. The angle measures in any quadrilateral always add up to 360°.

1.

30°

right 60°

2.
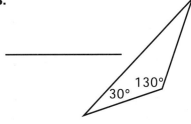
45°

25°

_____

3.
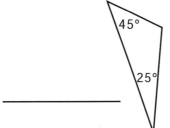
_____

30° 130°

4.
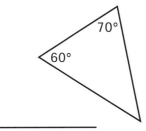
70°

60°

_____

5.
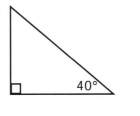
40°

_____

6.
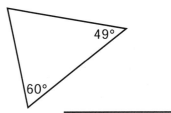
49°

60°

_____

DIRECTIONS: Find each missing angle measurement.

7.
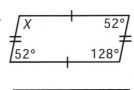
X

_____

8.
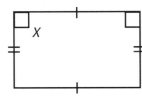
X   52°

52°   128°

_____

9.
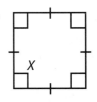
X

_____

10.
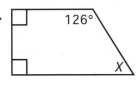
126°

X

_____

11.
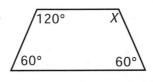
120°   X

60°   60°

_____

12.
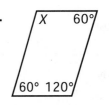
X   60°

60° 120°

_____

STOP

© Frank Schaffer Publications

Mathematics

6B.1 **Relationship Between Polygon** Use Geometric Methods
Vertices, Diagonals, and Sum of Its Angles

DIRECTIONS: Complete the table below.

Examples:

- To find the number of diagonals in a polygon, use the following formula: $n(n - 3) \div 2$.
- To find the number of interior triangles in a polygon, use the following formula: $n - 2$.
- To find the sum of the angles in a polygon, use the following formula: $t \times 180$.

  n = number of polygon sides
  t = number of interior triangles

 Clue — A **diagonal** is a line segment that connects nonadjacent vertices in a polygon.

Name	Sides	Diagonals	Interior Triangles	Sum of Angles
Quadrilateral				
Pentagon				
Hexagon				
Heptagon				
Octagon				
Nonagon				
Decagon				
Dodecagon				

STOP

© Frank Schaffer Publications

Mathematics

6B.2

Identifying Angles

DIRECTIONS: Choose the best answer. Use the shape below for questions 1–4.

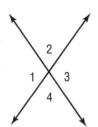

1. Angles 1 and 2 are _____ .

Ⓐ vertical

Ⓑ adjacent

2. Angles 1 and 3 are _____ .

Ⓕ vertical

Ⓖ adjacent

3. Angles 1 and 2 are _____ .

Ⓐ complementary

Ⓑ supplementary

Ⓒ equal

Ⓓ none of the above

4. Angles 1 and 3 are _____ .

Ⓕ complementary

Ⓖ supplementary

Ⓗ equal

Ⓙ none of the above

5. Supplementary means that the measure of two angles adds up to _____ .

Ⓐ 45°

Ⓑ 90°

Ⓒ 180°

Ⓓ 360°

6. Complementary means that the measure of two angles adds up to _____ .

Ⓕ 45°

Ⓖ 90°

Ⓗ 180°

Ⓙ 360°

7. Vertical angles are _____ .

Ⓐ complementary

Ⓑ supplementary

Ⓒ equal

Ⓓ none of the above

8. Adjacent angles are _____ .

Ⓕ complementary

Ⓖ supplementary

Ⓗ equal

Ⓙ none of the above

DIRECTIONS: Use the shape below for questions 9 and 10.

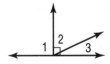

9. Angles 1 and 3 are _____ .

Ⓐ complementary

Ⓑ supplementary

Ⓒ equal

Ⓓ none of the above

10. Angles 2 and 3 are _____ .

Ⓕ complementary

Ⓖ supplementary

Ⓗ equal

Ⓙ none of the above

STOP

© Frank Schaffer Publications

Mathematics

6B.3

Analyzing Quadrilaterals

Use Geometric
Methods

DIRECTIONS: Complete the table below. In the *Description* column, describe the defining characteristics of the quadrilateral. In the *Name* column, identify the name of the quadrilateral.

Example	Description	Name

STOP

© Frank Schaffer Publications

Mathematics

6C.1

Making and Testing Conjectures

DIRECTIONS: Answer the following questions. If necessary, test your idea before answering by drawing various shapes.

 The length of any side of a triangle is less than or equal to the sum of the lengths of the other two sides. This is called **triangle inequality**.

1. **Can a triangle have the following measures: 4, 9, and 8? Explain.**

_____

_____

_____

_____

2. **Can a triangle have the following measures: 10, 18, and 7? Explain.**

_____

_____

_____

_____

 Complementary angles add up to 90°. Supplementary angles add up to 180°.

3. **In a parallelogram, are the adjacent angles complementary or supplementary? Write your answer, then draw a parallelogram and test your conjecture.**

_____

_____

_____

_____

4. **Which sides of a parallelogram ABCD are equal in length? Write your answer, then draw a parallelogram and test your conjecture.**

_____

_____

_____

_____

_____

STOP

© Frank Schaffer Publications

Mathematics

6C.2/6C.3

Justifying Theories About Angles

DIRECTIONS: Answer the following questions. If necessary, test your idea before answering by drawing various shapes.

Clue   The angles are identified with the symbol <.

1. **Examine the figure below. Use what you know about angles to prove that <1 = <2. Do not measure the angles. Complete the table below to help you find your answers. Fill in the missing formulas under the Statement column and the missing justifications under the Reason column. Some of the entries have been completed for you.**

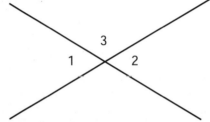

Statement	Reason
<1 + <3 = 180° <2 + <3 = 180°	
If the above statements are true, then:	Substitution
If the above statements are true, then:	Algebra

2. **Construct a triangle out of paper. Then cut off the corners and arrange them so that their angles meet at the vertex to form a straight line. What have you just proven? Explain your answer.**

_____

_____

_____

_____

STOP

© Frank Schaffer Publications

DIRECTIONS: Choose the best answer.

1. Angles 2 and 3 are
   _____ .

   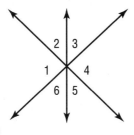

   Ⓐ   complementary
   Ⓑ   supplementary
   Ⓒ   equal
   Ⓓ   none of the above

2. If two angles are complementary and the
   measure of angle 1 is 26°, what is the measure
   of angle 2?

   Ⓕ   19°
   Ⓖ   64°
   Ⓗ   154°
   Ⓙ   334°

3. What is the missing measure in this triangle?

   Ⓐ   30°
   Ⓑ   50°
   Ⓒ   60°
   Ⓓ   90°

   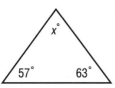

4. Draw and name a polygon with four sides and
   four right angles. Opposite sides are parallel.

5. The drawing shows parallelogram FGHJ with
   diagonal FH. Which angle is congruent to
   angle FGH?

   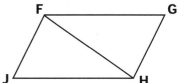

   Ⓕ   Angle FJH   Ⓗ   Angle FHG
   Ⓖ   Angle FHJ   Ⓙ   Angle GFJ

6. The sum of the measures of the angles in the
   above figure is _____ .

   Ⓐ   90°   Ⓒ   270°
   Ⓑ   180°   Ⓓ   360°

DIRECTIONS: Use the grid for questions 7–8.

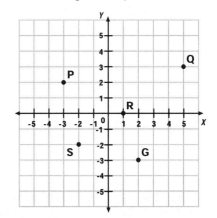

7. Which point is located at (−3, 2)?

   Ⓕ   R   Ⓗ   Q
   Ⓖ   G   Ⓙ   P

8. What are the coordinates for point G?

   Ⓐ   (1, 1)   Ⓒ   (−2, −2)
   Ⓑ   (2, −3)   Ⓓ   (−3, 2)

STOP

Mathematics Standards

Collect, Organize, and Analyze Data

Goal 7: Collect, organize, and analyze data using statistical methods; predict results; and interpret certainty using concepts of probability.

Learning Standard 7A—Students who meet the standard can organize, describe, and make predictions from existing data. *(Data Analysis)*
1. Construct, read, interpret, infer, predict, draw conclusions, and evaluate data from various displays, including circle graphs. *(See page 165.)*
2. Recognize and explain misleading displays of data due to inappropriate intervals on a scale. *(See page 166.)*

Learning Standard 7B—Students who meet the standard can formulate questions, design data collection methods, gather and analyze data, and communicate findings. *(Data Collection)*
1. Gather data by conducting simple simulations. *(See page 167.)*
2. Collect data over time with or without technology. *(See page 167.)*

Learning Standard 7C—Students who meet the standard can determine, describe, and apply the probabilities of events. *(Probability, including counting techniques)*
1. Record probabilities as fractions, decimals, or percents. *(See page 168.)*

What it means:
- **Probability** describes the chance that an uncertain event will occur.

2. Demonstrate that the sum of all probabilities equals one. *(See page 168.)*
3. Determine empirical probabilities from a set of data provided. *(See page 169.)*
4. Set up a simulation to model the probability of a single event. *(See page 170.)*
5. Discuss the effect of sample size on the empirical probability compared to the theoretical probability. *(See page 171.)*

What it means:
- **Empirical probability** is an estimate that an event will happen based on how often the event occurs after collecting data or running an experiment (in a large number of trials).
- **Theoretical probability** is the number of ways that an event can occur, divided by the total number of outcomes.

6. List outcomes by a variety of methods (e.g., tree diagram). *(See page 172.)*
7. Determine theoretical probabilities of simple events. *(See page 173.)*

© Frank Schaffer Publications

Evaluating Data

DIRECTIONS: Mr. Vandersy's class earned $582.00 during the school year in order to purchase new books for the library. The graph below shows the percentage of money earned from each activity. Use it to answer questions 1–3.

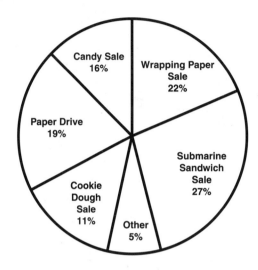

DIRECTIONS: The soccer team members needed to buy their own shin guards, socks, shoes, and shorts. Two players volunteered to do some comparative shopping to find the store with the best deals. Use their charts to answer questions 4–6.

Sam's Soccer Supplies
Socks . . . . 2 pairs for $6.84
Shoes . . . . 3 pairs for $84.15
Shin Guards . . . . 5 pairs for $35.70
Shorts . . . . 4 pairs for $36.36

Sports Corner
Socks . . . . 3 pairs for $9.30
Shoes . . . . 2 pairs for $48.24
Shin Guards . . . . .4 pairs for $32.48
Shorts . . . . 5 pairs for $60.30

1. **Which fund-raiser earned the most money?**

   (A) the candy sale

   (B) the wrapping paper sale

   (C) the submarine sandwich sale

   (D) the paper drive

2. **How much money was earned from the cookie dough sale?**

   (F) $63.02

   (G) $123.02

   (H) $64.02

   (J) $73.03

3. **How much less was earned on the paper drive than from the wrapping paper sale?**

   (A) $17.46

   (B) $23.46

   (C) $18.46

   (D) $16.46

4. **How much does it cost for one pair of shin guards at the store with the best deal?**

   (F) $7.14

   (G) $8.12

   (H) $32.48

   (J) $4.76

5. **How much would it cost to buy one pair of shoes and socks at Sports Corner?**

   (A) $27.22

   (B) $57.54

   (C) $31.47

   (D) $28.22

6. **How much would it cost to buy one pair of shoes and socks at Sam's Soccer Supplies?**

   (F) $27.22

   (G) $31.47

   (H) $29.11

   (J) $31.57

STOP

© Frank Schaffer Publications

Mathematics

7A.2

Recognizing
Misleading Displays of Data

Collect, Organize, and Analyze Data

DIRECTIONS: Answer the following questions based on the graph.

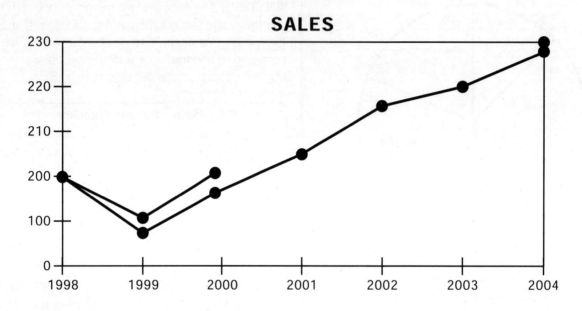

SALES

1. **Something is wrong with the y-axis on this graph. What is it?**

   _____

   _____

   _____

   _____

   _____

   _____

2. **What wrong impression might a person get from this graph if he or she does not look it carefully? Be specific.**

   _____

   _____

   _____

   _____

   _____

   _____

3. **How could this graph be fixed to present the data in a more usable way?**

   _____

   _____

   _____

   _____

   _____

   _____

   _____

STOP

© Frank Schaffer Publications

Mathematics

| 7B.1/7B.2 |

Collecting Data

DIRECTIONS: Answer in complete sentences.

1. If a survey is taken of students at a basketball camp, would the results be biased if the questions concern favorite sports? Explain.

   _____

   _____

   _____

2. Would the students at a basketball camp be a good sample population to represent a school's student population? Explain.

   _____

   _____

   _____

3. The entire sixth grade filled out a survey. Would this be a good sample population for a survey on favorite music of sixth graders? Explain.

   _____

   _____

   _____

4. Zoo visitors are asked their opinion on poaching. Is this a good sample population? Explain.

   _____

   _____

   _____

5. Bookstore visitors are asked their opinion on poaching. Is this a good sample population? Explain.

   _____

   _____

   _____

DIRECTIONS: Follow the instructions to gather data.

6. Take a single die and roll it 25 times. Record your results in the space below.

   Rolls of 1: _____

   Rolls of 2: _____

   Rolls of 3: _____

   Rolls of 4: _____

   Rolls of 5: _____

   Rolls of 6: _____

7. Each day for a week, take your pulse, run in place for one minute, then take your pulse again. Record the results below.

	Pulse rate before running	Pulse rate after running
Day 1		
Day 2		
Day 3		
Day 4		
Day 5		
Day 6		
Day 7		

STOP

Mathematics

7C.1/7C.2

Recording Probability

DIRECTIONS: Choose the best answer. For questions 1–4, suppose you wrote the word VACATION on a strip of paper and cut the paper into pieces with one letter per piece. If you put the pieces into a hat and pulled out one piece without looking, determine the probability of each situation.

1. **What is the probability that you would pick out the letter A?**

   (A) $\frac{1}{8}$

   (B) $\frac{2}{8}$

   (C) $\frac{4}{5}$

   (D) $\frac{2}{7}$

2. **Without returning the A to the hat, what is the probability that you would pick out the letter C?**

   (F) $\frac{1}{8}$

   (G) $\frac{1}{7}$

   (H) $\frac{2}{8}$

   (J) $\frac{1}{6}$

3. **Without returning the A or the C to the hat, what is the probability of picking a vowel?**

   (A) $\frac{4}{8}$

   (B) $\frac{3}{7}$

   (C) $\frac{3}{5}$

   (D) $\frac{3}{6}$

4. **Given the original word, what is the probability of picking a consonant?**

   (F) $\frac{1}{8}$

   (G) $\frac{4}{8}$

   (H) $\frac{2}{8}$

   (J) $\frac{4}{6}$

There are ten white tennis balls and ten green tennis balls in a box. Tony reaches into the box without looking.

5. **What is the probability that he will pick a white ball?**

   (A) 10%

   (B) 50%

   (C) 5%

   (D) 20%

6. **What is the probability that he will pick a green ball?**

   (F) 10%

   (G) 5%

   (H) 20%

   (J) 50%

DIRECTIONS: Follow the instructions to gather data.

7. **There are 2 red cards, 1 white card, 1 blue card, and 1 yellow card in a box. You reach into the box without looking. In decimal form, record the probabilities indicated below. The total should equal 1.00.**

   Probability that you will pick a red card: _____

   Probability that you will pick a white card: _____

   Probability that you will pick a blue card: _____

   Probability that you will pick a yellow card: _____

   TOTAL: 1.00

STOP

© Frank Schaffer Publications

Mathematics

7C.3

Determining
Empirical Probabilities

Collect, Organize,
and Analyze Data

DIRECTIONS: Choose the best answer.

The following are 2002 batting averages
for five Florida Marlins: Redmond, .305;
Floyd, .287; Lowell, .276; Owens, .270; and
Encarnacion, .262.

1. **How many hits would you expect Redmond to
   make out of the next 10 at bats?**

   (A) 305

   (B) 30

   (C) 3

   (D) .3

2. **How many hits would you expect Lowell to
   make out of the next 20 at bats?**

   (F) 276

   (G) 2.76

   (H) 3

   (J) 5

3. **What is Owen's batting average written as
   hits out of 100 attempts?**

   (A) .270

   (B) 27.0

   (C) 270

   (D) 2.70

4. **In 10 at bats, what would be the difference in
   hits between Redmond and Encarnacion?**

   (F) 3

   (G) 2

   (H) 1

   (J) 0

DIRECTIONS: Use the following data for questions 5–8.

About 7% of all Illinois drivers are teens.
Teens have 17% of all Illinois crashes. About
5% of U.S. drivers are teens. Teens have 15%
of all U.S. crashes.

5. **Out of 100 cars in a parking lot in Illinois,
   how many would you expect to be driven
   by teens?**

   (A) 7

   (B) 5

   (C) 15

   (D) 17

6. **Out of 100 cars in a parking lot in California,
   how many would you expect to be driven by
   teens?**

   (F) 7

   (G) 5

   (H) 15

   (J) 17

7. **If there were 200 accidents in Illinois in one
   month, how many would you expect to
   involve a teen?**

   (A) 14

   (B) 10

   (C) 30

   (D) 34

8. **If there were 200 accidents in Utah in one
   month, how many would you expect to
   involve a teen?**

   (F) 14

   (G) 10

   (H) 30

   (J) 34

STOP

© Frank Schaffer Publications

Name _____ Date _____

Modeling Probabilities

DIRECTIONS: Answer the following questions.

Empirical probability is an estimate that an event will happen based on how often the event occurs after collecting data or running an experiment. **Theoretical probability** is the number of ways that an event can occur, divided by the total number of outcomes.

1. **In a box there are 4 red crayons, 5 blue crayons, and 3 yellow crayons. If one crayon is chosen at random from the box, what is the theoretical probability of choosing a red crayon?**

   (A) $\frac{1}{12}$

   (B) $\frac{2}{3}$

   (C) $\frac{1}{3}$

   (D) $\frac{1}{2}$

2. **From the information in question 1, what is the theoretical probability of choosing a blue or yellow crayon?**

   (F) $\frac{1}{12}$

   (G) $\frac{2}{3}$

   (H) $\frac{1}{3}$

   (J) $\frac{1}{2}$

3. **Set up an experiment to model the situation in questions 1 and 2. (You may use other objects, such as marbles or colored bits of paper, if you cannot find enough crayons.) Perform the experiment and record your results below.**

Total number of choices	
Number of times red was chosen	
Number of times blue or yellow was chosen	

4. **From your experiment, record:**

   • the empirical probability of choosing a red crayon _____

   • the empirical probability of choosing a blue or yellow crayon _____

5. **Briefly describe any differences you found between your results and the theoretical probabilities of the events.**

   _____

   _____

   _____

   _____

   _____

   _____

   _____

   _____

   _____

   _____

   _____

   _____

   _____

© Frank Schaffer Publications

Name _____   Date _____

Mathematics

7C.5

Effect of Sample Size on Probabilities

DIRECTIONS: Answer the following questions.

1. What is the theoretical probability of randomly picking a face card from a standard 52-card deck?

   Ⓐ $\frac{1}{52}$

   Ⓑ $\frac{12}{52}$

   Ⓒ $\frac{2}{5}$

   Ⓓ $\frac{1}{2}$

2. Jose randomly picks a card from a standard 52-card deck and selects a 9 of hearts. He puts the card back into the deck and picks again. This time he selects the queen of clubs. From this experiment, he can predict that the empirical probability of randomly picking a face card from a standard 52-card deck is _____ .

   Ⓕ $\frac{1}{52}$

   Ⓖ $\frac{12}{52}$

   Ⓗ $\frac{2}{5}$

   Ⓙ $\frac{1}{2}$

3. Suppose instead of picking cards from the deck twice, as described in question 2, Jose picks cards 100 times. What do you think the effect will be on his prediction of the empirical probability of randomly picking a face card from the deck?

   _____

   _____

   _____

   _____

   _____

   _____

   _____

   _____

   _____

   _____

   _____

   _____

STOP

Mathematics

7C.6

Listing Outcomes

DIRECTIONS: Draw a tree diagram or make a list to show all the outcomes.

1. A new car can be ordered in black, red, or tan. You may also choose leather or fabric seats. Show the outcomes.

2. Phones come in two styles: wall and desk. They come in four colors: red, white, black, and beige. Show the outcomes.

3. The lunch room serves 3 types of fruit, 4 types of vegetables, and 2 types of meat. How many different combinations can be made from these choices? Draw the tree diagram to show all the outcomes.

4. Arapaho sees an ad in the newspaper for a sale at the Rain on Your Parade clothing store. Sundresses are selling for $35.88 each. Bonnets have dropped to the unbeatable price of 2 for $5.99, and sandals have slipped to $23.48 a pair. If Arapaho buys 2 sundresses, 6 bonnets, and three pairs of sandals, draw a tree diagram that shows how many outfits she can make with her purchases.

© Frank Schaffer Publications

Mathematics

7C.7

Determining Theoretical Probabilities

Collect, Organize, and Analyze Data

DIRECTIONS: Choose the best answer.

1. What is the probability of landing on a red section?

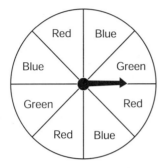

- (A) 1 out of 3
- (B) 2 out of 8
- (C) 5 out of 8
- (D) 3 out of 8

2. The game-show spinner below has 12 equal divisions. What is the probability that the pointer will land on a division worth more than $200 on the first spin?

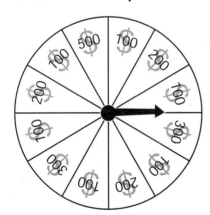

- (F) $\frac{1}{12}$
- (G) $\frac{1}{9}$
- (H) $\frac{1}{4}$
- (J) Not Here

3. What is the probability of rolling a number less than or equal to 3 on a dice?

- (A) $\frac{1}{2}$
- (B) $\frac{1}{12}$
- (C) $\frac{2}{3}$
- (D) $\frac{1}{6}$

4. Susan must draw a letter from a box that contains 6 A's, 7 B's, 4 C's, and 3 D's. Which of the following predictions is NOT accurate?

- (F) Susan will be more likely to draw an A than a C.
- (G) Susan will probably draw a D.
- (H) Susan will probably draw an A or a B.
- (J) Susan will be more likely to draw a B than a C.

5. It is _____ that she will draw a B than an A.

- (A) equally likely
- (B) less likely
- (C) more likely
- (D) not likely

6. A club has 9 girls and 6 boys. What is the probability that the club leader will ask a girl to lead the club in the singing of the traditional welcome song (assuming club members are called randomly to do this)?

- (F) 40%
- (G) 50%
- (H) 60%
- (J) 70%

STOP

© Frank Schaffer Publications

Mathematics

7

For pages 165–173

Mini-Test 5

Collect, Organize, and
Analyze Data

DIRECTIONS: The graph below shows the average basketball attendance for the season. Use the graph to answer questions 1–3.

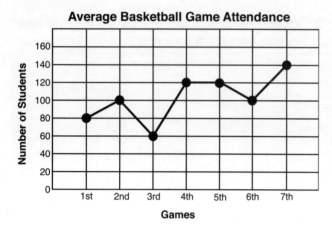

Average Basketball Game Attendance

1. **What was the increase in attendance from the first to the seventh game?**

    Ⓐ 50 students

    Ⓑ 60 students

    Ⓒ 140 students

    Ⓓ 70 students

2. **Between which two games was there the smallest increase in attendance?**

    Ⓕ 1st and 2nd games

    Ⓖ 6th and 7th games

    Ⓗ 5th and 6th games

    Ⓙ 2nd and 3rd games

3. **How many total students attended the games?**

    Ⓐ 140 students

    Ⓑ 160 students

    Ⓒ 720 students

    Ⓓ 600 students

4. **The sweaters on sale come in three styles: pullover, cardigan, and turtleneck. They come in three colors: black, white, and red. How many choices are there?**

    Ⓕ 9

    Ⓖ 6

    Ⓗ 3

    Ⓙ 12

5. **La Rue has a batting average of .249. How many hits should he have in the next 100 times at bat?**

    Ⓐ 249

    Ⓑ 25

    Ⓒ 3

    Ⓓ 10

6. **If you try to guess the month someone was born, what is the probability that you will guess the correct month?**

    Ⓕ $\frac{1}{12}$

    Ⓖ $\frac{1}{6}$

    Ⓗ $\frac{1}{24}$

    Ⓙ $\frac{1}{13}$

7. **Would asking individuals as they enter a mall be a good means of getting a random sampling for a survey on popular TV shows? Explain.**

    _____

    _____

    _____

    _____

STOP

© Frank Schaffer Publications

How Am I Doing?

Mini-Test 1

Page 129

Number Correct

[ ]

10–11 answers correct	**Great Job!** Move on to the section test on page 177.
7–9 answers correct	**You're almost there!** But you still need a little practice. Review the practice pages 111–128 before moving on to the section test on page 177.
0–6 answers correct	**Oops!** Time to review what you have learned and try again. Review the practice section on pages 111–128. Then retake the test on page 129. Now move on to the section test on page 177.

Mini-Test 2

Page 136

Number Correct

[ ]

7–8 answers correct	**Awesome!** Move on to the section test on page 177.
5–6 answers correct	**You're almost there!** But you still need a little practice. Review the practice pages 131–135 before moving on to the section test on page 177.
0–4 answers correct	**Oops!** Time to review what you have learned and try again. Review the practice section on pages 131–135. Then retake the test on page 136. Now move on to the section test on page 177.

Mini-Test 3

Page 150

Number Correct

[ ]

6 answers correct	**Great Job!** Move on to the section test on page 177.
4–5 answers correct	**You're almost there!** But you still need a little practice. Review the practice pages 139–149 before moving on to the section test on page 177.
0–3 answers correct	**Oops!** Time to review what you have learned and try again. Review the practice section on pages 139–149. Then retake the test on page 150. Now move on to the section test on page 177.

© Frank Schaffer Publications

How Am I Doing?

Mini-Test 4	7–8 answers correct	**Great Job!** Move on to the section test on page 177.
	5–6 answers correct	**You're almost there!** But you still need a little practice. Review the practice pages 153–162 before moving on to the section test on page 177.
Page 163 **Number Correct**	0–4 answers correct	**Oops!** Time to review what you have learned and try again. Review the practice section on pages 153–162. Then retake the test on page 163. Now move on to the section test on page 177.
Mini-Test 5	7 answers correct	**Awesome!** Move on to the section test on page 177.
	5–6 answers correct	**You're almost there!** But you still need a little practice. Review the practice pages 165–173 before moving on to the section test on page 177.
Page 174 **Number Correct**	0–4 answers correct	**Oops!** Time to review what you have learned and try again. Review the practice section on pages 165–173. Then retake the test on page 174. Now move on to the section test on page 177.

© Frank Schaffer Publications

Final Mathematics Test
for pages 111–173

DIRECTIONS: Choose the best answer.

1. **What is 7,000 in scientific notation?**
   - (A) 7×10^{12}
   - (B) 7×10^{9}
   - (C) 7×10^{6}
   - (D) 7×10^{3}

2. **Which sign best completes $\left|-1\right|$ ▪ $\frac{6}{7}$?**
   - (F) $>$
   - (G) $<$
   - (H) $=$
   - (J) Not Here

3. **Evaluate $5g + 2h$, if $g = 1$ and $h = 4$.**
   - (A) 13
   - (B) 28
   - (C) 22
   - (D) 7

4. **Fifteen percent of the students at Oakley Elementary are in sixth grade. There are 736 students in all. How many of them are in sixth grade?**
   - (F) 125
   - (G) 120
   - (H) 110
   - (J) 131

5. **Which of these is another way to write 4^{3}?**
   - (A) 4×3
   - (B) 12
   - (C) $4 \times 4 \times 4$
   - (D) $4 + 4 + 4$

6. **Sergio spent \$3.80 on heavy-duty string for his project. He bought 20 feet of string. Which number sentence could you use to find out the price per foot of the string?**
   - (F) $\$3.80 + 20 =$ ▪
   - (G) $\$3.80 - 20 =$ ▪
   - (H) $\$3.80 \times 20 =$ ▪
   - (J) $\$3.80 \div 20 =$ ▪

7. **If $x + 9 = 27$, then $x =$ _____ .**
   - (A) 3
   - (B) 16
   - (C) 36
   - (D) 18

8. **Evaluate $2m - 3n$, if $m = 5$ and $n = 2$.**
   - (F) 10
   - (G) 4
   - (H) 6
   - (J) 16

9. **A hiker started out with 48 ounces of water. She drank 9 ounces of water after hiking 5 miles and 16 more when she reached mile marker 8. How many ounces of water did she have left?**
   - (A) $48 - (9 + 16) = w$
   - (B) $48 + (9 - 16) = w$
   - (C) $(16 - 9) + 48 = w$
   - (D) $48 + (9 + 16) = w$

10. **A store is open for 12 hours a day. Each hour, an average of 15 customers come into the store. How many customers come into the store in a day?**
    - (F) $15 \times 24 = c$
    - (G) $12 + 15 = c$
    - (H) $12 \times 15 = c$
    - (J) $24 - 12 = c$

GO

© Frank Schaffer Publications

11. **Find the volume of a triangular prism with base = 7 yd., height = 7 yd., and length = 8 yd.**

  (A) 392 cubic yards

  (B) 98 cubic yards

  (C) 784 cubic yards

  (D) 196 cubic yards

12. **What is the volume of a rectangular prism with a length of 4 feet, a height of 2 feet, and a width of 1 foot?**

  (F) 16 cubic feet

  (G) 12 cubic feet

  (H) 8 cubic feet

  (J) 4 cubic feet

DIRECTIONS: Use the figure below for questions 13–17.

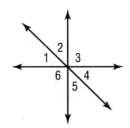

13. **Angles 1 and 4 are _____ .**

  (A) adjacent

  (B) vertical

14. **Angles 1 and 2 are _____ .**

  (F) adjacent

  (G) vertical

15. **Angles 1 and 4 are _____ .**

  (A) complementary

  (B) supplementary

  (C) equal

  (D) none of the above

16. **Angles 1 and 2 are _____ .**

  (F) complementary

  (G) supplementary

  (H) equal

  (J) none of the above

17. **Angles 3 and 6 are _____ .**

  (A) adjacent

  (B) vertical

18. **If angles 1 and 2 are complementary and the measure of angle 1 is 35°, what is the measure of angle 2?**

  (F) 10°

  (G) 55°

  (H) 145°

  (J) 325°

19. **Two of the angles in a triangle measure 48° and 87°. What is the measure of the third angle?**

  (A) 225°

  (B) 54°

  (C) 48°

  (D) 45°

20. **If angles 3 and 4 are supplementary and the measure of angle 3 is 124°, what is the measure of angle 4?**

  (F) 79°

  (G) 34°

  (H) 236°

  (J) 56°

DIRECTIONS: Use the figure below for questions 21–22.

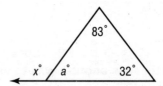

21. **Find the measure of a in the triangle.**

  (A) 115°

  (B) 65°

  (C) 13°

  (D) 245°

GO

© Frank Schaffer Publications

22. Find the measure of x in the figure.

    Ⓕ   115°

    Ⓖ   65°

    Ⓗ   13°

    Ⓙ   245°

23. The area of the triangle is _____ .

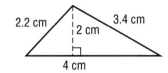

    Ⓐ 8 cm^2

    Ⓑ 4 cm^2

    Ⓒ 16 cm^2

    Ⓓ 9.6 cm^2

24. A circle has a diameter of 10 inches. Find the circumference.

    Ⓕ   3.14 inches

    Ⓖ   31.4 inches

    Ⓗ   15.7 inches

    Ⓙ   246.49 inches

DIRECTIONS: Write the measurement of the missing angle for questions 25 and 26.

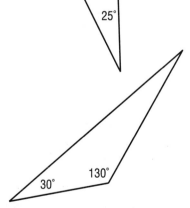

25.   Ⓐ   20°

         Ⓑ   310°

         Ⓒ   110°

         Ⓓ   70°

26.   Ⓕ   20°

         Ⓖ   100°

         Ⓗ   200°

         Ⓙ   160°

27. How many diagonals does an octagon have?

    Ⓐ   6

    Ⓑ   8

    Ⓒ   20

    Ⓓ   27

DIRECTIONS: Use the following paragraph for questions 28–31.

    Holly is in the process of redesigning the backyard landscape for her new house. In the design, she wants a square patio. Because she is still undecided about how large the patio should be, Holly changes her mind from time to time about the length of the sides of the patio.

28. Which of the following number patterns would represent the perimeter of the patio, in feet, if Holly changed the length of the sides from 3 feet to 4 feet to 5 feet?

    Ⓕ   9, 16, 25

    Ⓖ   12, 16, 20

    Ⓗ   4, 36, 49

    Ⓙ   3, 6, 10

29. Which of the following number patterns would represent the perimeter of the patio, in feet, if Holly changed the length of the sides from 4 feet to 5 feet to 6 feet?

    Ⓐ   9, 16, 25

    Ⓑ   4, 5, 6

    Ⓒ   16, 20, 24

    Ⓓ   16, 25, 36

30. Which of the following number patterns would represent the *area* of the patio, in square feet, if Holly changed the length of the sides from 3 feet to 4 feet to 5 feet?

    Ⓕ   12, 16, 20

    Ⓖ   9, 16, 25

    Ⓗ   16, 20, 24

    Ⓙ   16, 25, 36

31. Which of the following number patterns would represent the area of the patio, in square feet, if Holly changed the length of the sides from 5 feet to 6 feet to 7 feet?

    Ⓐ   25, 36, 49

    Ⓑ   15, 18, 21

    Ⓒ   16, 20, 24

    Ⓓ   20, 25, 36

GO ➡

32. Lucia is a great admirer of porcelain dolls, and she has a collection of brown-haired, blond-haired, and black-haired dolls. Her black-haired dolls outnumber her blond-haired dolls by a ratio of 3 to 1. She has 79 blond-haired dolls. How many black-haired dolls does Lucia have in her collection?

- (F) 82
- (G) 79
- (H) 158
- (J) 237

33. Line *A* is a graph of the equation $y = x + 1$. Which ordered pair below is a solution to the equation?

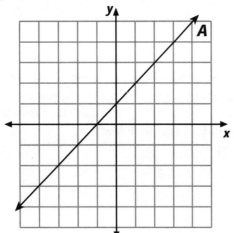

- (A) (2, 4)
- (B) (–2, 0)
- (C) (3, 4)
- (D) (–1, –1)

34. The ratio of walnuts to cashews in a certain nut mix is 3 to 7. If there are 49 cashews in the mix, how many walnuts are there?

- (F) 49
- (G) 112
- (H) 33
- (J) 21

35. A writing contest received 500 submissions. All 24 students in your class sent in a submission. What is the probability that someone in your class will win?

- (A) $\frac{1}{24}$
- (B) $\frac{1}{500}$
- (C) $\frac{6}{125}$
- (D) $\frac{1}{5}$

DIRECTIONS: The following data is a list of the monthly expenses (in percents) for the Whitt family. Use the data to answer questions 36–38.

Food:	15%	Transportation:	9%
Entertainment:	10%	Savings:	5%
Housing:	35%	Utilities:	8%
Miscellaneous:	12%	Clothing:	6%

36. If you were constructing a circle graph for the data above, which category would be represented by the largest part of the circle?

- (F) Food
- (G) Savings
- (H) Housing
- (J) Clothing

37. If you were constructing a circle graph for the data above, which category would be represented by the smallest part of the circle?

- (A) Savings
- (B) Clothing
- (C) Entertainment
- (D) Food

38. When constructing a circle graph for the data above, the part of the circle representing entertainment should be larger than the part representing which of the following expenses?

- (F) Food
- (G) Housing
- (H) Miscellaneous
- (J) Transportation

STOP

© Frank Schaffer Publications

Mathematics Test
Answer Sheet

1 Ⓐ Ⓑ Ⓒ Ⓓ   21 Ⓐ Ⓑ Ⓒ Ⓓ
2 Ⓕ Ⓖ Ⓗ Ⓙ   22 Ⓕ Ⓖ Ⓗ Ⓙ
3 Ⓐ Ⓑ Ⓒ Ⓓ   23 Ⓐ Ⓑ Ⓒ Ⓓ
4 Ⓕ Ⓖ Ⓗ Ⓙ   24 Ⓕ Ⓖ Ⓗ Ⓙ
5 Ⓐ Ⓑ Ⓒ Ⓓ   25 Ⓐ Ⓑ Ⓒ Ⓓ
6 Ⓕ Ⓖ Ⓗ Ⓙ   26 Ⓕ Ⓖ Ⓗ Ⓙ
7 Ⓐ Ⓑ Ⓒ Ⓓ   27 Ⓐ Ⓑ Ⓒ Ⓓ
8 Ⓕ Ⓖ Ⓗ Ⓙ   28 Ⓕ Ⓖ Ⓗ Ⓙ
9 Ⓐ Ⓑ Ⓒ Ⓓ   29 Ⓐ Ⓑ Ⓒ Ⓓ
10 Ⓕ Ⓖ Ⓗ Ⓙ   30 Ⓕ Ⓖ Ⓗ Ⓙ

11 Ⓐ Ⓑ Ⓒ Ⓓ   31 Ⓐ Ⓑ Ⓒ Ⓓ
12 Ⓕ Ⓖ Ⓗ Ⓙ   32 Ⓕ Ⓖ Ⓗ Ⓙ
13 Ⓐ Ⓑ   33 Ⓐ Ⓑ Ⓒ Ⓓ
14 Ⓕ Ⓖ   34 Ⓕ Ⓖ Ⓗ Ⓙ
15 Ⓐ Ⓑ Ⓒ Ⓓ   35 Ⓐ Ⓑ Ⓒ Ⓓ
16 Ⓕ Ⓖ Ⓗ Ⓙ   36 Ⓕ Ⓖ Ⓗ Ⓙ
17 Ⓐ Ⓑ   37 Ⓐ Ⓑ Ⓒ Ⓓ
18 Ⓕ Ⓖ Ⓗ Ⓙ   38 Ⓕ Ⓖ Ⓗ Ⓙ
19 Ⓐ Ⓑ Ⓒ Ⓓ
20 Ⓕ Ⓖ Ⓗ Ⓙ

© Frank Schaffer Publications

Answer Key

Page 8
1. D
2. G
3. B
4. F
5. C
6. H
7. D
8. G
9. D

Page 9
1. prearranged
2. overprotective
3. distrust
4. nonconformist
5. deface
6. undervalue
7. interlock
8. postgraduate
9. inconsiderate
10. redesign

11–20. Answers may vary. Sample answers are given.
11. pregame
12. defuse
13. interfaith
14. nonfat
15. renew
16. underage
17. dislike
18. overpay
19. postscript
20. inability

Pages 10–11
1. C
2. G
3. C
4. H
5. B
6. G
7. A
8. J
9. C
10. G
11. C
12. F
13. A

14. F
15. B
16. G
17. D
18. G
19. D
20. G

Page 12
1. antique
2. wonderful
3. unique
4. reminded
5. interesting
6. discussing
7. petite
8. angry
9. soggy
10. cheap
11. starving
12. disasters

Page 13
1. You have nothing to say.
2. Someone is very happy.
3. Someone is really special.
4. Answers will vary.

Page 14
1. foolish
2. century
3. cloudless
4. ordinary
5. red
6. land
7. permit
8. melody
9. stop
10. light
11. come
12. positive
13. lass
14. untidy
15. lengthy
16. enjoy

Page 15
1. B
2. J
3. A
4. H
5. C
6. F
7. A
8. J

Pages 16–17
1. B
2. F
3. C
4. J
5. C
6. H
7. expenditures— what you spend your money on; debit—items you subtract from your income; credit—items you add to your income; cash flow —relationship between debits and credits; the amount you spend. Sentences will vary.

Page 18
1. zooming
2. plink
3. rustling
4. the park
5. Answers will vary. Possible answer: "Wait for me, Brian" and "Sit here and eat, and don't move until I come back to get you."
6. Answers will vary. Possible answer: Brian parked his bike and followed his nose to the concession stand.

Page 19 Mini-Test 1
1. B
2. G
3. D
4. F
5. D
6. J
7. C
8. G

Page 21
1. B
2. H
3. B
4. G

Pages 22–23
1. D
2. J
3. A
4. H
5. B
6. F
7. B

Pages 24–25
1. Antarctica: extreme cold; little or no vegetation, not much animal life Sahara: extreme heat; lack of water and vegetation; limited animal life
2. Antarctica: humans live in buildings protected from extreme temperatures; animals live near coasts where they can find food in the ocean Sahara: humans move from place to place and live in tents, some irrigate the land; animals have

© Frank Schaffer Publications

adapted to the heat and lack of water; for example, the camel can store large amounts of water in its body
3. Students should list several reasons why they would choose to visit either Antarctica or the Sahara.

Pages 26–27
1. B
2. H
3. A
4. J
5. B
6. F

Page 28
1. M
2. S
3. M
4. S
5. S
6. M
7. M
8. M

Pages 29–30
1. Students should mention where the elephant lives (savanna or forest) and which tusk the elephant favors.
2. Students should mention the possibility that the elephants would have been killed off.
3. A poacher is someone who kills animals illegally.
4. Students should mention that it became more difficult to sell ivory, so it was harder to make money as a poacher.

5. If the ivory trade were made legal, more elephants would be killed.
6. Students should mention some of the conservation efforts discussed in the passage.
7. Answers will vary. One possible answer: World Wildlife Federation, because this organization is involved in preserving animal species.
8. Answers will vary. One possible answer: The jaguar, which is often hunted for its fur.

Page 31
1. Hawaii
2. around a month
3. girl
4. parrot (or other exotic bird)
5. Canada
6. soccer

Pages 32–33
1. 100-meter dash
2. long jump
3. shot put
4. high jump
5. 400-meter run
6. 110-meter hurdles
7. discus throw
8. pole vault
9. javelin throw
10. 1,500-meter run
11. discus throw
12. 100-meter dash
13. pole vault
14. high jump
15. 1,500-meter run
16. shot put
17. 110-meter hurdles

18. javelin
19. long jump
20. 400-meter run

Pages 34–35
1. D
2. F
3. C
4. H
5. A
6. G
7. A
8. Answers will vary. Possible answer: The art shows an old "horseless carriage," which signals that the article will likely discuss early automobiles.

Pages 36–37
1. Robin is polite.
   A. She says "thank you."
   B. She brings a hostess gift.
2. Sheila is greedy.
   A. She grabs the candy.
   B. She asks for milk.
3. Tamiko is fearful.
   A. She wants to call her parents.
   B. She brought a flashlight and a teddy bear.
4. Paula is rude.
   A. She asks if her boyfriend can come over.
   B. She rolls her eyes.
5. Ted is mischievous.
   A. He is wearing a mask.
   B. He plans to scare the girls.

Page 38
1. Answers may vary. Possible answer: The s sounds in the line sound like waves of the sea swelling and crashing.
2. B
3. Answers will vary. Possible answer: The images are a bit difficult to understand, as love can sometimes be.
4. F

Pages 39–40
1. B; Mr. Chan tells the students to be quiet and sit at their desks.
2. F; She was eager to share her story. She thought it was a good one.
3. B; The students lined up and went outside. A fire truck came to the school.
4. G; They arrived in a fire truck and carried a water hose.
5. A; A puff of smoke came out of a window near the cafeteria.
6. The cafeteria wasn't safe because there was damage from smoke.

Pages 41–42
1. B
2. G
3. A
4. G
5. A
6. J
7. C

Pages 43–44

1. A. squirrel, adoring; B. rabbit, practical
2. A squirrel wants a rabbit to leave her burrow, marry him, and live with him in the trees; she refuses.
3. Answers will vary. One possible answer is "the value of knowing where you belong."
4. hopeful, lovesick
5. annoyed, realistic
6. The squirrel describes his home as far above the rabbit's home in the warren.
7. The rabbit lives in a sheltered hollow, from which she can reach gardens with carrots and cabbages. The squirrel lives up in the trees.

Page 45

1–4. Be sure that students understand what each of the categories (fiction, nonfiction, biography, and poetry) means.
5. Students should mention traits unique to each type of book.
6. Students should mention traits the books have in common.
7. Be sure students offer some support for their opinions.

Pages 46–47
Mini-Test 2

1. A
2. H
3. B
4. J
5. A
6. J

Pages 49–50

Note: Answers are given for the "After Reading" column. Answers will vary in the "Before Reading" column.

1. O
2. F
3. O
4. O
5. F
6. O
7. F
8. F
9. F
10. O
11. F
12. O
13. Answers will vary. Students should support their predictions with facts from the article.

Page 51

1. C
2. Answers will vary. Possible answer: People brought picnics to watch a battle.
3. J
4. Answers will vary: Possible answer: What was predicted to be an easy victory for the Union forces turned into a rout.

Pages 52–53

1. Answers will vary. Possible answer: Robinson felt grateful to Rickey for giving him a chance to play in the major leagues.
2. Answers will vary. Possible answer: Segregation prevented many talented black baseball players from achieving the fame and income they would have achieved had they been allowed to play in the major leagues.
3. Answers will vary: Possible answer: Robinson felt proud and happy about his accomplishments.
4. Answers will vary. Possible answers: Who were some teammates who came to Robinson's defense? How did other baseball owners react to Branch Rickey's decision to allow Robinson to play for the Dodgers?

Page 54

1. B
2. A
3. B
4. B
5. A
6. C
7. D
8. D
9. C
10. B
11. A
12. C

Pages 55–56

1. A
2. J
3. D
4. G
5. C
6. G
7. B

Page 57

Answers may vary to all questions. Suggested answers follow.

1. Skim through the TV guide quickly until you find Friday at 8:00, then read that section closely.
2. Consult the index and look up *Spiders*.
3. Pay close attention to every detail in the recipe.
4. Read an entire article or book about Kennedy, paying close attention to what you read.
5. Create a graphic organizer, listing the rules for American football on one side and the rules for Canadian football on the other side.

Pages 58–59

Answers will vary to all questions. Suggested answers follow.

1. Person who likes racing: Bill loves to race and will keep at it. Person who dislikes racing: Bill loves to race but has a lot to learn.

© Frank Schaffer Publications

2. Person who likes racing: determined, exciting
Person who dislikes racing: foolish, reckless
3. Person who likes racing: Bill should keep racing.
Person who dislikes racing: Bill should go to college.
4. Person who likes racing: It is an exciting sport to participate in and watch.
Person who dislikes racing: It is a sport that is too risky and dangerous.

Pages 60–61
I. A. rescues dogs from animal shelters
B. trains dogs
C. educates the public on the need for these dogs
II. A. hearing impaired
B. physically challenged
C. multiple handicapped
III. A. basic obedience
1. "sit"
2. "come"
3. "down"
B. sound-alert training
1. respond to six sounds
2. training geared to needs
C. home placement training
1. bonding with owner
2. getting familiar with routines
IV. Answers will vary.

Page 62
1. B
2. Answers will vary. Possible answer: The grass is "speaking" like a person in the poem *Grass*.
3. The fog is compared to a cat. Students' responses will vary.
4. Answers will vary. Students may state that the imagery in the poem "Fog" is easier to understand because it uses simpler language.

Page 63
1. Answers will vary. Possible answer: Even though the United States was attacked on September 11, 2001, the country will endure.
2. Answers will vary. Possible answer: The illustrator was confident and resolute that the country would survive. You can tell because the flag is the predominant image, not the burning buildings.

Page 64
1. Answers will vary. Students should tell how the book review would influence their decisions to read or not read the book.
2–3. Answers will vary.

Pages 65-66
1. D
2. F
3. B
4. G
5. D
6. H
7. D
8. J

Pages 67–68
Mini-Test 3
1. D
2. H
3. B
4. G
5. C
6. G
7. B

Page 70
1. sandpaper
2. the cat and the electric sander
3. No. Free-verse poems often break lines in the middle of sentences.
4. A sharp bit of twig stuck in her fur.
5. Answers will vary.

Pages 71–72
1. The narrator is Winona, who is reading her speech to her dad.
2. B
3. H
4. Dad suggests that Winona rethink the point of the speech and make it more logical.
5. Answers will vary. Students should state how the story might be different if another person narrated the story.

Page 73
Tate
How he feels before the game—excited; it's the championship game.
What he does during the game—hits a home run.
What he probably does next—gets another ice cream cone. (Answers will vary.)
Jeffrey
How he feels before the game—nervous; he's been in a batting slump.
What he does during the game—hits the winning run.
What he probably does next—buys Tate another cone.
Alyssa
How she feels before the game—calm and confident; it's her nature.
What she does during the game—stays cool and pitches well.
What she probably does next—enjoys the team's victory.

Pages 74–75
1. C
2. G
Answers will vary to questions 3–5. Suggested answers follow.
3. Both stories are about friends enjoying their time together.
4. Both stories contain characters who have been friends a long time and who know each other well.

5. Cathy and Stacey seem a bit more imaginative and perhaps athletic than Will and Scott.

Pages 76–77
Setting—Philadelphia
Main Characters—the brave little black-eyed rebel; the boy selling apples and potatoes
Plot—problem: She wanted to bring letters to the wives and children of the soldiers.
Plot—goal: The goal is to secretly pass the letters from the boy to the girl.
Episodes—(1) The boy came to the market. (2) The girl pretended to trade a kiss for a dozen apples. (3) The boy passed the letters to the girl.
Climax—The girl puts her arms around his neck in front of a watching crowd.
Resolution—He put the letters under her shawl, and she delivered them to waiting loved ones.

Page 78
Students' stories will vary but should include the following words: kaleidoscope, spiral/spiraled, translucent, manipulate/manipulating, turbulent, fray/frayed, spy/spied, reluctantly.

Pages 79–80
1. play
2. poem
3. fable
4. B
5. H
6. A
7. J

8. B
9. myth
10. science fiction
11. realistic fiction
12. nonfiction

Pages 81–82
1. D
2. H
3. A
4. G
5. B
6. H

Page 83
1. C
2. F
3. C
4. H
5. C
6. H
7. D

Pages 84–85
Mini-Test 4
1. B
2. J
3. C
4. H
5. D
6. F
7. B
8. Answers will vary. Possible answer: The story might show a daughter helping a mother pack possessions and load them into a moving van for a move across the country. As they work, the mother and daughter recall memories of the various objects they are packing.

Pages 87–88
1. K
2. E
3. F
4. B
5. D
6. I
7. H
8. J

9. A
10. G
11. M
12. L
13. C
14. B
15. G
16. A

Page 89
Students' answers will vary. Students should describe their three favorite genres and, for each, name their favorite authors and works (including a brief summary). They should also tell which authors they have read the most and why.

Page 90
1. C
2. Answers will vary. Possible answers: The speaker awoke "six miles from earth"; the speaker awoke to "black flak" (artillery fire).
3. J
4. B

Pages 91–92
1. A
2. G
3. C
4. H
5. D
6. J
7. Answers will vary.

Page 93
Answers will vary. Students should select important issues of the day and find or watch three different stories about them. Students should describe the subjects of the stories, tell the main facts regarding the issues, find points of agreement/disagreement among the stories, identify different details each story might contain, and evaluate the tone of each story.

Page 94
Students' responses will vary. Brief descriptions of the historical works follow.
- Beowulf—Old English epic poem
- Anansie tales—West Indian/African folktales
- The Twenty-Two Goblins—Indian folklore series
- The Two Frogs—Japanese folktale
- The Nose—Russian short story
- A Modest Proposal—Irish satirical essay
- The Animals Sick of the Plague—French fable
- Ode on a Grecian Urn—English poem

Pages 95–96
1. Answers will vary. Possible answer: The narrator is about 12 years old. The way he speaks and the things he does are typical of 12-year-old boys.
2. A
3. Answers will vary. The narrator says, "This time, I was thinking. No more broken windows." He obviously thought he had found a way to play ball without hurting anything.
4. F
5. Answers will vary. The narrator says, "I'm in trouble again," so the incident must

© Frank Schaffer Publications

have happened fairly recently. The concluding two paragraphs also indicate that he hasn't yet made restitution to Mrs. Banter, again suggesting that the incident is recent.

6. Answers will vary.

Page 97

1. ran—dashed, darted, sprinted, bolted, rushed, flew, raced, charged
2. screamed—shouted, yelled, bellowed, roared, cheered
3. Answers will vary regarding how the word choice enhances the story. Possible answer: The different words present slightly different images; "running" is not the same as "dashing" or "darting," for instance. The words also help clarify the character's personality; the reader gets a certain mental image of someone who "bellows" as opposed to someone who "hoarsely shouts."

Pages 98–99

1. Narrator goes fishing and falls into water.
2. Narrator goes to archery class and hits another camper's target.

3. Narrator goes to camping-skills class and spills stew into fire.
4. Narrator goes to bed in cabin.
5. Narrator sees a big shadow.
6. a big owl
7. by not telling us what the shadow is; by asking the various questions
8. Answers will vary. Possible answer: A big owl, just as the narrator had been describing.

Page 100 Mini-Test 5

1. B
2. J
3. B
4. Answers will vary. Students should retell the Daedalus myth using the nonfiction passage for information. Students should write in the style and tone of a fable or folktale. This style generally includes a moral at the end.

Pages 103–106 Final Reading Test

1. C
2. G
3. D
4. H
5. D
6. G
7. A
8. H
9. D
10. H
11. C
12. H
13. A
14. G
15. C
16. F

17. A
18. H
19. A
20. H
21. D
22. J
23. C
24. G

Page 111

1. B
2. F
3. C
4. H
5. A
6. G
7. A
8. H

Page 112

1. D
2. H
3. D
4. G
5. C
6. H
7. C
8. G
9.

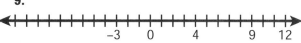

Page 113

1. A
2. J
3. C
4. F

Page 114

1. B
2. H
3. A
4. F
5. C
6. H
7. A
8. G

Page 115

1. C
2. F
3. B
4. J
5. B
6. G
7. A
8. J
9. B

Page 116

1. $2 \times 2 \times 5 \times 5$
2. $2 \times 3 \times 5 \times 7$
3. $2 \times 2 \times 11$
4. $2 \times 3 \times 5 \times 5 \times 7$

Page 117

1. A
2. H
3. C
4. G
5. C
6. J
7. A
8. H

Page 118

1. C
2. H
3. D
4. F
5. B
6. H

© Frank Schaffer Publications

187

Page 119
1. B
2. F
3. C
4. F
5. B
6. H
7. D

Page 120
1. C
2. F
3. C
4. G
5. A
6. J

Page 121
1. C
2. F
3. C
4. G
5. A
6. F
7. C

Page 122
1. 8
2. 25
3. 27
4. 72
5. 32
6. 3
7. 8^2 or 4^3 or 2^6
8. 10^2
9. 5^2
10. 5^3
11. 4^2 or 2^4
12. 3^5
13. 6^3
14. 9^3 or 3^6
15. 7^3
16. 2,456.9
17. 590
18. 615,892
19. 23.4
20. 68,000
21. 5,349,800

Page 123
1. B
2. H
3. D
4. J
5. B
6. F

Page 124
1. B
2. H
3. D
4. G
5. A
6. H

Page 125
1. 9 of the diamonds should be shaded.
2. 12 of the bullets should be shaded.
3. 8 of the arrows should be shaded.
4. 20%
5. 62.5%
6. 80%
7. 33%
8. 80%
9. 10%
10. Yes. Stocks can more than double in price.
11. No. Prices cannot go below 0.

Page 126
1. C
2. H
3. B
4. H
5. C
6. F
7. C

Page 127
1. Y
2. N
3. N
4. Y
5. N
6. Y
7. N
8. N

Page 128
1. B
2. G
3. C
4. G
5. B
6. F
7. C

Page 129 Mini-Test 1
1. D
2. G
3. B
4. F
5. B
6. J
7. B
8. G
9. C
10. G

Page 131
1. A
2. H
3. B
4. G

Page 132
1. D
2. F
3. C
4. H
5. C
6. F

Page 133
1. 4 cm^2
2. 3.6 m^2
3. 3.525 in.^{2}
4. 48 ft.^{2}
5. 2.7 yd.^{2}
6. 5.1 dm^2

Page 134
1. A
2. G
3. D
4. H
5. A
6. G
7. C
8. H
9. B

Page 135
1. C = 25.12 in.
   A = 50.24 in.^{2}
2. C = 314 mm
   A = 7850 mm^2
3. C = 9.42 in.
   A = 7.065 in.^{2}
4. C = 62.8 ft.
   A = 314 ft.^{2}
5. C = 5.024 cm
   A = 2.0096 cm^2
6. C = 3.14 mm
   A = 0.785 mm^2
7. 17.444 mm
8. 11.775 in.
9. 0.366 m

Page 136 Mini-Test 2
1. D
2. F
3. D
4. H
5. A
6. G
7. C
8. J

Page 139
1. D
2. J
3. C
4. G
5. C

Page 140
1. C
2. J
3. A
4. H
5. A
6. H
7. A

Page 141
1. A
2. H
3. B
4. H
5. B
6. G
7. B

Page 142
1. D
2. G
3. B
4. H
5. A
6. F
7. C
8. J

© Frank Schaffer Publications

Page 143

1.

2.

3.

4.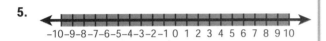

5.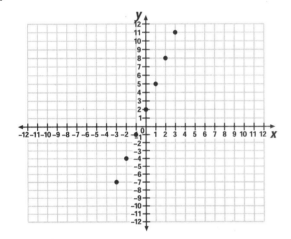

Page 144

1.

x	−3	−2	−1	0	1	2	3
y	−7	−4	−1	2	5	8	11

2.

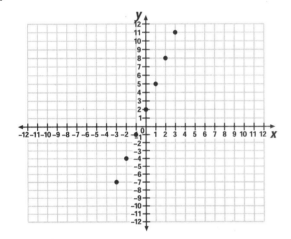

3.

x	−3	−2	−1	0	1	2	3
y	−6	−4	−2	0	2	4	6

4.

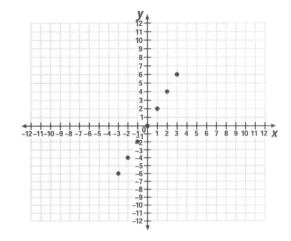

Page 145
1. C
2. F
3. B
4. G
5. C

Page 146
1. According to the order of operations, multiplication must be performed first, then addition. Therefore, the order of the numbers in the problem is crucial and cannot be changed.
2. The communicative property holds only for addition and multiplication, not subtraction and division.
3. B
4. H
5. D
6. G

Page 147
1. Y
2. N
3. Y
4. Y
5. N
6. N
7. N
8. Y
9. N
10. −
11. +
12. ÷
13. ×
14. −7
15. + 15
16. −3
17. ÷ 7
18. + 34
19. × 9
20. ÷ 2

Page 148
Students' choice of variables.
1. *Variable:*
Let c = number of cookies left
Number sentence:
c + 5 = 12

© Frank Schaffer Publications

Model: Students' models should illustrate the equation and solution.
Solution: c = 7

2. *Variable:*
Let d = amount Austin earned
Number sentence:
d − 2 = 8
Model: Students' models should illustrate the equation and solution.
Solution: d = 10

3. *Variable:*
Let x = number of CDs Logan brought
Number sentence:
x ÷ 3 = 3
Model: Students' models should illustrate the equation and solution.
Solution: x = 9

Page 149
1. B
2. G
3. B
4. J
5. B
6. G
7. B
8. G
9. D

Page 150 Mini-Test 3
1. C
2. F
3. A
4. F
5. C
6. F

Page 153
1. D
2. F
3. B
4. H
5. A
6.

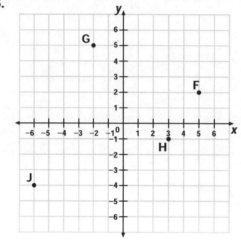

Page 154
1. Reflection across y-axis
2. Translation 8 units left and 2 units down
3. Reflection across y-axis
4. Reflection across x-axis
5. Translation 6 units right and 8 units down
6. Translation 3 units down

Page 155
1.

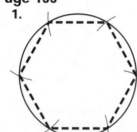

2.

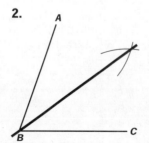

3.

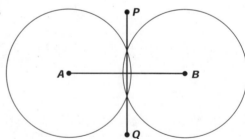

Page 156
1. B
2. J
3. C
4. F
5. B

Page 157
1. acute 60°
2. obtuse 110°
3. acute 20°
4. acute 50°
5. right 50°
6. acute 71°
7. 90°
8. 128°
9. 90°
10. 54°
11. 120°
12. 120°

© Frank Schaffer Publications

Page 158

Name	Sides	Diagonals	Interior triangles	Sum of angles
Quadrilateral	4	2	2	360°
Pentagon	5	5	3	540°
Hexagon	6	9	4	720°
Heptagon	7	14	5	900°
Octagon	8	20	6	1080°
Nonagon	9	27	7	1260°
Decagon	10	35	8	1440°
Dodecagon	12	54	10	1800°

Page 159
1. B
2. F
3. B
4. H
5. C
6. G
7. C
8. J
9. D
10. F

Page 160

Students' descriptions may vary but should generally include the information given on the right.

Example	Description	Name
	One pair of opposite sides are parallel	trapezoid
	Opposite sides are parallel and opposite sides and opposite angles are congruent	parallelogram
	Parallelogram with all sides congruent	rhombus
	Parallelogram with four right angles	rectangle
	Rectangle with four congruent sides	square

Page 161
1. According to triangle inequality, the length of any side of a triangle is less than or equal to the sum of the lengths of the other two sides. Therefore, this set of measures can form a triangle because 4 + 9 is greater than 8; 9 + 8 is greater than 4; and 4 + 8 is greater than 9.
2. This set of measures cannot form a triangle because 10 + 7 is less than 18, which violates triangle inequality.
3. Adjacent angles in a parallelogram are supplementary.
4. Opposite sides of a parallelogram are equal in length. In this case, AD = BC and AB = CD.

Page 162

1.

Statement	Reason
<1 + <3 = 180° <2 + <3 = 180°	A straight angle measures exactly 180°
If the statements above are true, then: <1 + <3 = < 2 + <3	Substitution
If the statements above are true, then: <1 = <2	Algebra

2. You have proven that the sum of the angles of a triangle is 180 degrees. By following the instructions, you have used the angles of the triangle to form a straight line, which equals 180 degrees.

Page 163 Mini-Test 4

1. A
2. G
3. C
4. square

5. F
6. D
7. J
8. B

Page 165

1. C
2. H
3. A
4. F
5. A
6. G

Page 166

1. The intervals on the y-axis are inconsistent. From 0 to 200, they rise in intervals of 100; then they suddenly begin rising only in intervals of 10.
2. The $30.00 increase between 2000 and 2004 appears greater than the $100.00 decrease between 1998 and 1999.
3. The intervals on the y-axis should be redone consistently, perhaps in intervals of 50.

Page 167

1. Yes, it would be biased because the students like basketball.
2. No. It is probably mostly athletic students.
3. Yes, this is a good sample because it includes the entire population of one school.

4. No. Most zoo visitors are concerned for animals and are knowledgeable about the impact of poaching on the environment.
5. Yes. This would be a diverse sampling of people.
6. Students' results will vary. They are to take a single die, roll it 25 times, and record the results.
7. Students' results will vary. They are to take their pulse, run in place for one minute, than take their pulse again and record the results.

Page 168

1. B
2. G
3. D
4. G
5. B
6. J
7. Probability that you will pick a red card: 0.40
Probability that you will pick a white card: 0.20
Probability that you will pick a blue card: 0.20
Probability that you will pick a yellow card: 0.20

Page 169

1. C
2. J
3. B
4. H
5. A
6. G
7. D
8. H

Page 170

1. C
2. G
3. Students' answers will vary. They are to randomly select 4 red crayons, 5 blue crayons, and 3 yellow crayons from a box and record the results.
4. Students' answers will vary based largely on the number of times they choose a crayon.
5. Students' answers will vary based largely on the number of times they choose a crayon. The more times they choose, the closer their empirical probabilities will resemble the theoretical probabilities.

Page 171

1. B
2. J
3. Students' answers will vary but should generally state that increasing the sample size (i.e., picking cards 100 times rather than 2 times) should cause Jose's prediction of the empirical probability to more closely resemble the theoretical probability of $\frac{12}{52}$.

© Frank Schaffer Publications

Page 172

Students are to show probability outcomes for a number of situations. They may choose several different ways to show the outcomes. Sample answers below illustrate the outcomes as tree diagrams.

1.

2.

3.

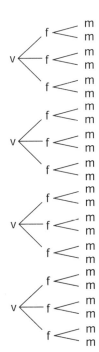

4.

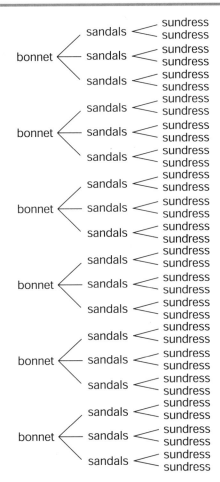

Page 173

1. D
2. H
3. A
4. G
5. C
6. H

Page 174 Mini-Test 5

1. B
2. F
3. C
4. F
5. B
6. F
7. Yes, as long as it is done throughout the day so that there is a variety of age groups surveyed.

Pages 177-180 Final Mathematics Test

1. D
2. F
3. A
4. H
5. C
6. J
7. D
8. G
9. A
10. H
11. D
12. H
13. B
14. F
15. C
16. F
17. B
18. G
19. D
20. J
21. B
22. F
23. B
24. G
25. C
26. F
27. C
28. G
29. C
30. G
31. A
32. J
33. C
34. J
35. C
36. H
37. A
38. J

NOTES

© Frank Schaffer Publications

NOTES

© Frank Schaffer Publications

NOTES

© Frank Schaffer Publications

NOTES

© Frank Schaffer Publications

NOTES

© Frank Schaffer Publications

NOTES

© Frank Schaffer Publications

NOTES

© Frank Schaffer Publications